Lillian Walker

Washington State Civil Rights Pioneer

A Biography & Oral History

by John C. Hughes

THE WASHINGTON STATE
HERITAGE CENTER

LEGACY PROJECT

First Edition
Copyright © 2010

Washington State Legacy Project
Office of the Secretary of State
All rights reserved.
ISBN 978-1-889320-22-9
Front cover photo: Metcalf Studo, Harrisburg, Illinois
Book Design by Kathryn E. Campbell
Printed in the United States of America
by Gorham Printing, Centralia, Washington

Washington
Secretary of State
SAM REED

DEDICATION

For Dianne Robinson, Robin Hunt,
Sam Reed and John Hughes,
who have kept history alive,
and my grandchildren,
who need to carry it on.

—LILLIAN WALKER

EDITOR'S NOTE

In this oral history, Lillian Walker candidly shares the profoundly offensive racial epithets she encountered growing up, particularly in the early years of the civil rights struggle in Kitsap County. What some prefer to call the "N-Word" is mentioned several times. She also discusses her concern over its use by blacks themselves, including her own mother. She has devoted her life to "educating people" about the evils of racism. If you are a parent or teacher sharing her inspiring story with young people, you may want to consider emphasizing the historical context of the epithets and develop class protocols for a discussion of hate and hateful words. Teachers might also consider having students read the oral history before the biography, then have a class discussion on how the historian developed the biography from the interviews.

Lillian around 1940 when she left Illinois to come to the Northwest.

*"I knew someone had to take the first step and
I made up my mind not to move (to the back of the bus)....
I would like to be known as a person who is concerned about
freedom and equality and justice and prosperity for all people."*

—**Rosa Parks, 1913-2005**

A sign like this was in many Bremerton
businesses in the 1940s. *Library of Congress*

I t was 1944, the apex of World War II, and the Navy was keeping an eye on its Negroes. Some 4,000 worked at the bustling Bremerton Shipyard and other military installations along the Kitsap Peninsula on Washington's Puget Sound. They were angry because many businesses, including cafes, taverns, drug stores and barber shops, displayed signs saying, "We Cater to White Trade Only." Before the war, only about 100 blacks lived in Bremerton. The newcomers had come from all over, especially the South and the industrial cities of the North, happy to have jobs and expecting to leave Jim Crow behind. Many racists made the same trip, however, joining earlier transplants and home-grown bigots. The Ku Klux Klan's revival in the 1920s recruited thousands in the Pacific Northwest. Captivated by Nativist mumbo-jumbo, they donned their bed-sheet robes, paraded around flaming crosses and railed against Catholics, Jews, Negroes, Asians, "mongrel" immigrants and union activists.

Lillian Walker, whose husband James worked at the shipyard, was the recording secretary of the Puget Sound Civic Society, a civil rights coalition formed by the newly chartered Bremerton branch of the National Association for the Advancement of Colored People. She was 31 years old and flabbergasted that prejudice was so prevalent in a place where the air was clean and "everything was green." She always said, "You're either with me or against me. And if you're against me, that means we're going to have to fight!"

She was still in the trenches in 2009, the NAACP's centennial year. Her new hip was an aggravation, but at 96 she was as spunky as ever and checking her e-mail regularly. When Lillian was young, she dreamed of becoming a doctor. Unfortunately, she was born the wrong color and the wrong gender at the wrong time in the wrong place. Still, she harbors no bitterness over the fact that she and James had to take on an assortment of part-time janitorial jobs for 40 years to make ends meet and give their children a better life. If you visit the bathroom in her home, Mrs. Walker will ask with a mischievous smile if you took note of the sign over the sink. It says, "You have a right to your opinion just as long as it agrees with mine!" A former bookkeeper, her house is filled with photos, plaques and mementoes. She's still cooking on a 1947 Tappan Deluxe range. Every element and the oven are in good working order and she's annoyed that she can't find someone to fix the clock. "Why are you always smiling?" someone once asked. "Frowning and cursing," she replied, "that's not going to make you any friends." Lillian Walker has been "educating people," as she puts it, about racial equality for as long as she can remember, and she remembers 1944 vividly. That was the year she helped found the Bremerton branch of the NAACP. After some false starts, the civil rights movement in Kitsap County began to get traction.

The Civic Society was organized in the summer of '43, according to a confidential report on the "Negro Situation" submitted to the Navy Yard commandant on March 6, 1944. Other declassified documents indicate the Navy was worried that communists and radical unionists could be infiltrating the group and stirring up trouble. Robert D. Addison, the group's president, worked at the shipyard. He agreed to talk with the Navy investigators

Shipyard workers lining up for lunch during World War II. *Kitsap County Historical Museum*

and "stated that from his observations the majority of the negroes are highly dissatisfied and very much disillusioned because of existing discrimination. He pointed out that these colored workers have come here at the request of the government and the majority of them feel the government should make a greater effort to make conditions more pleasant."

The Navy sent informants to a mass meeting sponsored by the Civic Society. The guest speaker was Charles M. Stokes, a Negro attorney from Seattle who was on the threshold of a remarkable career. Stokes called the whites-only signs wartime "morale sabotage" and "particularly stressed the fact that white and colored people should be treated equally." He urged the "approximately 250 colored persons" who attended the meeting to protest discrimination in "an orderly and courteous manner." But if they were still refused service by Bremerton businessmen, Stokes left "the impression that he would be willing to take the matter to court to make a test case."

Impatient, some blacks took matters into their own hands, the Navy Intelligence Office noted. The Bremerton Police Department advised that on the night of February 6, 1944, "a maroon colored Dodge sedan containing a number of negroes was being driven around town with the occupants throwing rooks (sic) at the windows of establishments displaying such signs. Windows were broken at the Beach Cafe, Pop's Inn Tavern, and the In and Out Cafe." Moreover, on February 18, 1944, Ozona Bonner, a black woman employed as a sweeper at the Navy Yard, had slapped Ruth

Green, a white employee, in the women's locker room of Building 495. "It was reported that this negro woman was standing in a crowded aisle when the white woman, carrying a number of packages, passed through, bumping into her, following which the negro woman struck the white woman in the face, causing her nose to bleed. For this act, the negress was suspended for three days." Lillian Walker has always tried to live "the Christian life," but she wouldn't have turned the other cheek either, and if they had suspended her for three days, Attorney Stokes would have been on the first ferry from Seattle.

In 1944, Lillian's score was far and away the highest on the postal clerk exam and she was appointed postmaster at Sinclair Park, the hilltop housing project for black Navy Yard workers. Then she gave up the prospect of a bright career with the Postal Service to have children. "My going places was lesser (important) than being a mom," she says. "I wanted to raise my kids. I wanted to instill me in them, not somebody else teaching them what they wanted to be." Exhibit A would be her son, James T. Walker Jr., Ph.D. A Stanford graduate, he is an epidemiologist with the Centers for Disease Control in Cincinnati.

Although she claims she keeps forgetting things, they are rarely very important. She does crossword puzzles, loves Scrabble and recalls addresses and other facts with the facility of someone 40 years younger. She is tough, too, and for several years walked around with appendicitis. She treated it with icepacks, a trick she learned during her days as a nurse in a rural clinic. She won three bouts with diphtheria, three more with pneumonia and endured 22 radiation treatments for uterine cancer in 1982, using "humor therapy"—"I Love Lucy" and the Marx Brothers—to stay on the sunny side. She lost three children, including twins, in pregnancy but sublimated her grief with her gumption and zest for life. She is an icon in her community, with a host of friends who love and revere her. Her congressman says she personifies community spirit; candidates all want their signs in her yard.

Lillian Walker never expected to live this long. In fact, she took Social

Security early at 62. "Sometimes now I ask God, 'What are you keeping me here for?' And God says, 'You're doing it.' And I say, 'What am I doing?' 'Well,' He says, 'you're nice to everybody.' But I tell Him, 'I've always been nice to people.' " Besides being nice, she is wise. She has been alive for nearly a century of American history and made history. There have been 17 presidents in her lifetime, from Woodrow Wilson to Barack Obama. She met the 32nd, Franklin D. Roosevelt, and was fighting for civil rights when Martin Luther King was in Junior High.

Dirt poor but proud

With an itinerant midwife and her grandmother assisting, Lillian was born at 4:30 a.m. on October 2, 1913, in a shack on a 20-acre farm near Carrier Mills in rural Illinois. Her parents, Moses and Hazel Allen, were both of mixed race, "mulattoes" in the parlance of the Census. Dad worked some of the time as a coal miner, but most of the time as a farmer. The Allen home was without electricity. Water came from a pump on the porch. The outhouse was out back—"way out back." When the Depression hit in '29, they were already so poor—"dirt poor," as they used to say—they hardly noticed. Like her siblings, Lillian learned early on to plant, plough and hoe,

Lewis, Ulysses and Lillian Allen with Jack the dog at the Allen family home in the 1930s.

milk the cow, slop the pig, gather the eggs, chop kindling and rustle up something for the stew pot. By 9, she could plunk a wild rabbit with a .22 rifle. She walked barefoot to a two-room school that housed grades one through eight. High school was three miles farther down the road but the only time she got a ride was when it snowed hard. Dad would then harness the horse and take her on the buckboard. Her parents insisted that they all go to school. "You didn't dare miss a day. We didn't play hooky, and in my family if you got a whipping at school, you got a whipping at home."

Her mother suffered a blow to the head at the hands of her stepfather for some perceived insolence when she was in the fourth grade and was never able to read after that. She would have Lillian read aloud to her from the newspaper, magazines or books while she cooked supper. Forty years later, after she and Moses moved to Washington State, Hazel Allen was featured in a *Seattle Post-Intelligencer* article about Bremerton's literacy program. An accompanying photo shows her listening intently to a tutor, still striving to learn to read. She could proudly write her name and "count money" like a champ because she kept close track of her egg sales. Lillian got her persistence from her mother.

Shirley and Mary Allen, Lillian's older siblings. The little girl died of burns after playing too close to the fireplace.

In all, Lillian's folks had 11 children, six of whom died young. Poor little Mary suffered horrible burns after playing too close to the fire; Charles was 2 or 3 years old and sleeping in the same bed with Lillian when he awoke choking. They put a spoon in his mouth to try to clear the airway, but the toddler died before the doctor traversed the 12 miles from Harrisburg. A few years later, Lillian was "so excited to have a little sister," but Juanita lived only a few hours. Flora Belle succumbed to an unremembered childhood illness and William died of measles. Next came Brenda Iris, who died in infancy. Happily, the last, James Franklin, survived childhood. "Lord knows, life was hard," Lillian says. "Think of my poor mother. But they were never negative! Mom always encouraged us, and Dad always said, 'You can do anything anybody else can do.' And I always said, 'I can do anything you can do, only I can do it better.' "

Lillian isn't sure how these two formidable ladies fit in her family tree, but the photo says a lot about her ancestors.

As to color, some of the fascinating faces in Mrs. Walker's family album look white. Others range from clearly to vaguely African-American, although all are light-skinned, like Lillian. Her father's mother, Grandma Elvira Allen, was mixed-race, the granddaughter of a Tennessee slave owner. According to family lore, his daughter's husband departed the plantation, possibly to deal in slaves, and never returned. The daughter lapsed into an illicit relationship with "a Portuguese man who lived on the plantation." He may have been a slave or himself a slave trader. The clear inference is that he was not white and calling him Portuguese may have been an attempt to sanitize the scandal. Portugal once had a far-flung colonial empire and in the mid-1400s began importing thousands of black slaves, many of whom in due course intermarried with whites. It was one of the world's leading slave traders until late in the 18th Century.

The plantation owner, meantime, was also enduring financial problems, presumably as the Civil War storm clouds gathered. He was tempted to sell his daughter's eight illegitimate children as slaves. "Fearing this action by her father," the story goes, she and her "Portuguese" partner fled to Illinois, where they could live free and homestead. There, they were married, some 20 years after they first met. Their daughter, Elvira, born in 1849—12 years before the start of the Civil War—grew to young womanhood near the

Lillian's grandmother, Elvira Allen, around the turn of the century with two young relatives.

colored community of Lakeview. It was a wide spot in the road where free blacks had settled, a dusty mile from Carrier Mills. Willis Allen was her second husband. We know little of his lineage except that he had a black father and a white mother. Lillian has a photo of Grandma Elvira, long-necked and dressed in black but looking white. She offers a thin smile and melancholy eyes. She's posing with a beautiful young mixed-race woman and a curly-haired black boy who looks to be about a year old. Mrs. Walker has forgotten the identities of the young woman and child, but surmises that it's a generational photo—grandma with a great-grandchild and a grandchild or niece.

A Depression-era photo of Mrs. Walker's parents is an American Gothic classic. If one picture is worth a thousand words, this one speaks volumes. Hazel Allen, a hefty, salt-of-the-earth character in a house dress, has her right arm affectionately draped over Moses' shoulder. He's wearing a hat, a white shirt, a go-to-church tie and his best trousers, hiked up by suspenders. "Mose" and Hazel were often mistaken for white. It's easy to see why.

Moses and Hazel Allen, Lillian's parents.

Lillian's late husband, James T. Walker Sr., a shipyard electronics inspector, was the grandson of slaves who "jumped over the broom" to formalize their marriage in Virginia. (Some scholars believe the tradition is rooted in African symbolism.) When he heard that Lincoln had signed the Emancipation Proclamation, James' grandfather exclaimed, "Now I'm a man!"

In her lifetime, Lillian Allen Walker has seen America move from lynching Negroes to electing them to its highest offices. Through it all, she has never stopped wondering why race matters. "I don't see *color*," she says. "I see each person as an individual." To paraphrase a quip by President Obama, she sees herself as an All-American "mutt" and she's proud of it.

A fighter

Mrs. Walker signed on as a custodian at the Bremerton Navy Yard in 1941. A woman in Personnel insisted on giving her two ID badges, one Filipino, one white, because she wasn't sure what race she was. With all due respect to Filipinos—and Caucasians—that struck Lillian as preposterous. "I told her I was a Negro—that I wasn't going to wear a Filipino badge. People

This Puget Sound Naval Shipyard ID badge belonged to Lillian's dear friend, Marie Greer. *Black Historical Society of Kitsap County*

told me, 'You could have passed (for white).' But why should I? I've always been proud to be who I am. I'm color blind. I tell people, I have as many white friends as I have black friends. I've always tried to treat people like I want to be treated. I don't care what color you are as long as you're a good person. I've never understood prejudice, and I've never put up with it." On a trip to Louisiana in the 1940s to visit her husband's relatives, she nearly lost it. "I had gone to the store to buy a pair of hose, and the clerk stopped waiting on me when a white person came in," Lillian recalls. Furious, she stomped out of the store and simmered in the car until James returned from his own errands. The look on her face spelled trouble. "Would you get me out of this town," she implored, "because otherwise I'm going to kill somebody?" A few years later after they'd won some desegregation battles in the courtroom, she was more confident. James came home from the shipyard one night and said the Navy wanted to send him down South for a while "but I hate to take you down there, honey." "Don't worry about that," Lillian said. "We'll either straighten out the town or we'll move!"

As fate would have it, the Walkers stayed to straighten out Bremerton. James, quieter but just as persistent, was with Lillian every inch of the way as they fought discrimination and worked on multiple fronts to make it a better city. If they had moved South, they surely would have been in the thick of the brutal civil rights struggles there, marching with Dr. King and staging sit-ins. Kindred souls, Lillian Walker and Rosa Parks were born the same year. Anyone who has met Lillian can easily imagine her on that bus in Montgomery, Alabama, on that fateful day in 1955 when Rosa refused to surrender her seat to a white man. Lillian and Rosa were both active in the African Methodist Episcopal Church. They resemble one another physically as well. But Lillian Walker, a spitfire when provoked, might have socked the bus driver had he dared lay a hand on her.

Growing up, the three pillars of Lillian's life were home, school and church. The Allens preferred the Baptist Church or the Methodist Church over the Holy Sanctified Church, a Pentecostal movement born among slaves. The Sanctified parishioners were prone to shouting out their joy as the spirit moved them. Lillian's faith has always been deep and abiding but she gets irked by "hollering and shouting because you can't understand what the preacher's saying." They always wore their Sunday best to church. "We'd walk barefoot up to church, and take towels to clean our feet," she recalls. "We would sit down on the church lawn and put our shoes on and then we'd go inside." At mid-week, they'd be back for Bible Study.

After Grandma Elvira died, Grandpa Willis Allen came to live with Lillian's family. In the summertime, the kids were charged with keeping

Grandma Elvira and Grandpa Willis Allen, who came to live with
Lillian's family after his wife died.

Lillian Allen (face circled) with the students and teachers at the tiny rural school in the 1920s.

the flies off him as he sat on the porch in the lethargy of elderliness. One day he slumped over from a stroke and the children ran inside to declare, "There's something wrong with grandpa!" The doctor came as soon as he could. "Grandpa lasted about three days and then he was gone," Lillian recalls. Poor people were familiar with the fragility of life and weren't given to complaining. Folk remedies treated a myriad of ailments. "If we had a toothache, and if it had a hollow in it, Dad would either put a piece of carbide in it—you know, what the coal miners used—or pull it because we couldn't afford a dentist."

In Illinois back then, "You couldn't go to school until you were 7." Lillian could hardly wait. Then, because her birthday is in October, they told her she had to wait until she was nearly 8. She read books by the light of a kerosene lamp at the "study table." When she was in the third grade, she and her brothers were the only colored kids. One day, a white girl named Helen called her a nigger. Lillian calmly handed her books to a white chum, Dimple Edwards, and bopped Helen in the nose. Helen never again called her a nigger. In fact, they became best friends. Nor was there any boy "that dare tackle me or say something nasty to me because I'd beat him. I was raised with brothers and we rassled." She was smart, too. When she was promoted to ninth grade in 1930, her teachers noted that her work was "exceptional" in every subject.

Harrisburg, where her father worked sporadically at the coal mine, was about a dozen miles away. On Fridays, Mom, Dad and the kids would pick vegetables—"beans, peas, potatoes, whatever"—and Dad would take the produce to town to sell. He'd often stay overnight at the miners' bunkhouse." One Saturday

Hazel and Moses Allen at their home near Carrier Mills, Illinois in 1940.

evening, he arrived back home with a buckboard full of produce. He hadn't sold anything. "People just don't have any money," he said, shaking his head. "That was the first time that I realized there was a Depression," Lillian says. "We didn't realize we were poor." They ate some of the vegetables, canned the rest and were thankful they weren't hungry. At Christmas, each child might get an orange or new pair of socks Mom had knit.

Practical nursing

After graduation from Carrier Mills High School, Lillian knew "we couldn't afford college." If she couldn't be a doctor she at least wanted to be a nurse. She was hired at the 13-bed Lewis Home Sanitorium in Harrisburg and worked her way up from flunky to ad hoc anesthesiologist, taking correspondence courses in nursing. Skeptical at first that she just wanted to earn money to buy Easter clothes, J.H. Lewis, the black physician who owned the clinic, soon realized Lillian had a natural aptitude for medicine. She wasn't the least bit squeamish about blood and other bodily fluids. Surgery fascinated her. She learned to handle every increasingly important task with painstaking attention to detail. Friends would ask, "Doesn't the blood bother you?" And she'd say, "They could cut your head open, and then go and sew it back on. It's fine with me." One day they brought in a young man who had been practically scalped in an automobile accident. Lillian was unfazed as they methodically cleaned the wound and sewed his scalp back on. The doctor was impressed. "He was a good teacher," Lillian recalls, "and I really got training. The only time that I messed up was one time when I was giving ether to a patient. 'Breathe in, breathe out, breathe in,' I said, and the ether put *me* to sleep. I learned after that that you don't breathe when you're giving ether!"

When she departed for Chicago after two and a half years, Dr. Lewis gave her a glowing letter of reference: She "performed her duties very satisfactorily," including "practical nursing, office assistant, cooking, dietetics, urinalysis, taking blood pressure, assisting in operations, either giving ether or serving in capacity of operative assistant" as well as overseeing post-operative care. "She has demonstrated a willingness to work hard and a fine type of intelligence, which coupled with her natural interest in medical work, should fit her for a successful career in nursing."

It was in 1937 that she went to live with her father's sister, Aunt Carrie, and work for a family as a nurse and maid. She delighted in the bustle of the huge city and loved going to museums and "all the educational things." Then she met a young musician with a thousand-watt smile: James Titus Walker. He was raised by his grandmother in Future City, Illinois, a suburb—to use that word loosely—of Cairo. Future City was falling way short of living up to its name, and Cairo was a Mississippi River town where racism was rampant. James left town after the 10th grade to live in Louisiana with his mother and his stepfather, who taught him to play the saxophone. After completing high school, James joined his stepfather's five-piece band. A naturally talented musician, he ended up traveling widely before landing in Chicago. They were a handsome couple. James was 27, Lillian 25. He was quiet but quick-witted. She was confident and assertive. He loved her and she loved him, but every time he asked her to marry him she said no: "I'm not going to marry a musician. I am not going to starve to death!"

"Well, honey," he promised, "I'm looking for another job."

Come 1940, James' mother was living in Seattle, where Boeing and the shipyards were beginning to mobilize. While pledging "your boys are not going to be sent into any foreign wars," President Roosevelt was transforming the U.S. into "The Arsenal of Democracy" to aid Great Britain as the Nazis subjugated Europe. Japan was also on the march. James arrived in Seattle that November and lined up the promise of a job at the Navy Yard or Ammunitions Depot in Bremerton by spring. He found work as a laborer at an Army storage depot for $6 a day, signed up for the Merchant Marines, just in case, and sent for Lillian. A well-to-do couple in Longview needed a gardener, chauffeur, cook and maid. James and Lillian filled the bill and worked there until May when the Navy called. They were married in Seattle and arrived in Bremerton on June 20, 1941, with everything they owned in a shopping bag. Nannie Jones, a black lady, had a room for rent.

Welcome to Bremerton

The tough old Navy town was on the threshold of stunning growth and culture shock. Bremerton's population zoomed from 15,000 in 1940 to 75,000 by 1944, elevating it to the state's fourth largest city. The newcomers were pitching tents, sleeping in cars, on park benches, even in chicken coops. Shipyard workers coming off the graveyard shift were bumping others out of boarding-house bunks. They called it "hot bedding." It was so crowded in Bremerton that many workers commuted from Seattle on the *Kalakala*, the legendary streamlined ferry that looked like something out of a Flash Gordon serial. Seattle grew from 368,000 to 530,000 in the same time

The *Kalakala* passes the Bremerton Navy Yard en route to Seattle in the 1940s.

period. In all, some 600,000 migrants flocked to Washington's cities and towns to do war work, thousands of them blacks from the South and urban East and Midwest. Uncle Sam poured $40 billion into the West Coast. Per capita income in the state soared, even with 41 percent population growth factored in.

World War II did what all of the Roosevelt Administration's alphabet agencies—the NRA, WPA, TVA and CCC—couldn't achieve: It ended the Great Depression. It also changed the face of the Evergreen State, demographically and industrially. "Between Pearl Harbor and VJ day in August of 1945, the industrial framework of Washington took its modern form," Robert E. Ficken and Charles P. LeWarne note in *Washington, A Centennial History*. "Employees of sawmills and logging camps declined from 46 percent of the workforce in 1939 to 17 percent in 1944. In revealing contrast, shipyard employment increased from 1 percent to 32 percent."

Bremerton was home to about 100 blacks in 1940, according to the U.S. Census. By the summer of 1944, 4,600 were working for the military at the Navy Yard, the Ammunitions Depot and the Torpedo Station. Uncle Sam had a far better track record of hiring blacks than Boeing or the civilian shipyards. Dianne Robinson, a Bremerton City Council member who is the founder and curator of the Black Historical Society of Kitsap County, believes there were actually upwards of 10,000 blacks in the county at the peak of the war—as many as in Seattle. The Census data is of little use because the war fell between its enumerations in 1940 and 1950 and the yearly estimates lack demographics. In any case, Robinson doesn't trust black demographic data from that era. "At one time, black people wouldn't even talk to Census people, or they would give them really negative (or misleading) information. They were afraid to really say how many people there were in a household. Not only that, but we have to include blacks in the military stationed in Kitsap County and the workers' families."

A hastily formed housing authority steered the blacks recruited by the Navy into segregated projects—Sinclair Heights in Bremerton and Orchard Heights in Port Orchard. There were about 280 black housing units in all, plus the "Duration Dormitories" for single workers. Once unpacked,

Shipyard workers lived in trailers and tents in 1942. *Puget Sound Navy Museum*

black workers promptly wrote to family and friends from Florida to Texas, thousands of whom headed for Puget Sound. "I know of three families that lived in one side of one of those duplex units," Robinson says. "That's how they did it. Family and friends followed the workers who arrived, all of them coming for an opportunity to make some money. They were really packed into a lot of those units."

Especially for blacks bogged down in the South, World War II provided an opportunity to enter the workforce, learn a trade and lead better lives. Most who headed West, including Lillian and James Walker, never imagined they would encounter racism in what seemed to be a land of opportunity. Trade unions also resisted integration; never mind that there was a war on. The Aeronautical Mechanics Union local and Boeing management stonewalled the hiring of blacks—and white women—despite the growing need for war workers and President Roosevelt's 1941 executive order calling for fair employment practices in labor and industry, historian Polly Reed Myers has documented. Union men feared that white female and minority membership would "bring down wages and hinder union effectiveness." Blacks and whites worked together with less animus at the

Bremerton Navy Yard, but the Negroes there knew that moving up to plum jobs would be tough.

Racial tension in defense industries and the migration of job-seeking blacks to cities sparked race riots in 1943 in several American cities, including Los Angeles. One of the shades-of-gray ironies is that blacks from the North were sometimes critical of blacks who arrived in the Northwest from the Deep South. In Bremerton, some whites drew that distinction, too, maintaining that the Southern Negroes—accustomed to more prejudice and generally less educated—were often rude or otherwise uncouth, just "not as nice" as the other Negroes. Mrs. Walker says she saw some of that herself and remembers shaking her head at the newcomers' bad manners.

Growing pains

The bigots in Bremerton were a vocal minority, part of the shipyard city's wartime growing pains, but there were a lot more than a handful. Bremerton had been a rough and tumble town practically from its birth at the turn of the century, with a "notoriously loose moral tradition." In 1942, it was over-dosing on testosterone and cheap beer. Six dance pavilions, a dozen brothels, miscellaneous freelance hookers and hundreds of proverbial drunken sailors crowding taverns and tattoo parlors added up to relentless trouble. The Police Department had a dozen men in 1940 and 54 at war's end. Often that wasn't nearly enough, *The Kitsap Sun* recalled in 2001 when the city observed its centennial. "Stories of people being robbed on the streets and public fights made news on a daily basis by 1945....That year, 400 sailors 'rioted' in a 'near mob scene' near the ferry terminal... and it took 12 officers to subdue the melee, the result of a series of fights." Teenage girls had a 10 p.m. curfew, and Police Chief Art Morken "regularly warned the populace of the dangers of unattended adolescents, who often had both parents working, or a mom at work and a dad overseas."

The good news was that when the black folks began to assert themselves some righteous white people joined the cause. One was the Walkers' neighbor, Ron Johnson. He had a gun that he vowed to use if anyone attacked Jim and Lillian for daring to expect equality. Another was Peggy Gustafson, who stood shoulder to shoulder with Lillian when she was refused service at a downtown cafe. Chief Morken is also fondly remembered by Bremerton's longtime black residents but he had his hands full. His crowded town never slept. When Sinclair Heights and four other federally-financed housing projects were annexed to the city in 1943, the chief had another 16,000 citizens to

Bremerton police chief Art Morken, left, with the chief of the Navy Shore Patrol during World War II.

serve and protect and miles more turf to patrol. Morken had advanced from traffic cop to captain in the space of seven years and was named acting chief in 1942 at the age of 33 when Chief Charles "Slats" Lewis went off to war. The average age of the department was 31. To deal with the volatile night-life downtown, Bremerton Police "have gone back to an era almost forgotten when night sticks were badges of authority," *Sheriff & Police Repo*rter magazine noted in 1943. "The department has one of the state's most serious traffic situations, the result of narrow streets and the thousands of war workers who, three times daily, pour in and out of the Navy Yard. During peak traffic hours, 15 officers are assigned to principal intersections to alleviate the congestion." In the midst of all that, Morken was affable and fair-minded—"a very nice white man," according to Mrs. Walker. He earned their enduring respect by prodding business owners to realize that with so many blacks arriving in town, racism was not only wrong, it was going to hit them in the pocketbook. Ed Bremer, whose German immigrant father founded the city at the turn of the century, did what he could to help, opening a beer parlor called The Casino especially

A front page from a 1940 edition of Seattle's leading black newspaper.
The Walkers helped with its circulation in the Kitsap County area.

for blacks. It offered food, drinks and dancing—"a place where you could go and feel comfortable," Lillian says.

James and Lillian worked at the black USO Club in the Labor Temple, one of the few places with a welcome sign for Negro servicemen. Racism was rampant in the military and the Shore Patrol and shipyard guards often looked the other way. In March of 1945, *The Northwest Herald*, a black newspaper in Seattle, reported that two black defense workers in Bremerton had been chased out of the New China cafe by five Marines. "[T]hey proceeded to beat and abuse Junior Howard, who was not fortunate enough to escape them as the other. When he was finally loosened" they spotted Edward Barnett, another resident of the nearby black dormitory. They "caught up to him just outside the Navy Yard gate.…In plain view of the guards on the gate, the Marines, who by this time had increased to seven, beat him, crushing his eyeglasses, giving him an ugly cut over his eye and breaking a bottle of liquor on his back…They then disappeared through the gate into the Navy Yard. Barnett had to have nine stitches taken." The paper headlined the story "Nazism in Bremerton."

One morning, utterly without provocation, two sailors jumped James Walker. Lillian was janitoring inside the Tower Theater and James was mopping the entrance. Another "real good cop," Officer Ben White, happened by and collared the attackers, who sputtered that he must be a "nigger lover." Woolworth's lunch counter in downtown Bremerton also discriminated against blacks into the 1950s and was the site of NAACP sit-ins. "Bremerton was a white supremacist town," Mrs. Walker says. "I'd never experienced anything in Illinois like we encountered when we came here."

Civil rights law, meantime, was a paper tiger in Washington State. The 1890 Legislature, imbued with Populism and recoiling from the virulent anti-Chinese riots of the mid-1880s, passed a Public Accommodations Act that granted "all persons within the State of Washington…of whatever race, color or nationality…full and equal enjoyment" of hotels, theaters and restaurants, as well as trains, boats and coaches. Infractions were punishable by fines ranging from $50 to $300 or 30 days to six months in jail. However, the 1895 Legislature turned conservative in the wake of The Panic of '93, which hit America every bit as hard as the recession of 2008-10. It

The Black USO Club at the Labor Temple in downtown Bremerton during World War II.
Black Historical Society of Kitsap County

removed the penalties from the Public Accommodations Act. The move went largely unchallenged for years because prior to World War II, there had been few Negroes in Washington State—2,500 at the turn of the century and still only 7,400 in 1940. When the throng of newcomers to Puget Sound encountered racism, they mobilized. James and Lillian Walker and their dear friends, Elwood and Marie Greer, Loxie and Alyce Eagans and Gertrude Joseph were indefatigable NAACP members.

In the 1940s, the Triangle Café near the entrance to the Navy Yard was the scene of a notable sit-in, actually a "stand-outside." After an NAACP meeting, Lillian, her friend Peggy Gustafson and another white lady stopped for a bite to eat. When they sat down at the counter, the waitress asked the white women what they'd like, pointedly ignoring Lillian. Peggy nodded toward Lillian. "I'll have whatever Mrs. Walker is having." Lillian piped up that she'd like a piece of pie and a cup of coffee. The waitress promptly ducked around the corner. Lillian gave chase.

"I told you I wanted a piece of pie and a cup of coffee."

"Well, I've only got two hands!"

Ulysses Allen, Lillian's younger brother. He came to live with Lillian and James in Bremerton during the 1940s.

"You're not using either one of them. What's your name and your phone number? And what's your boss's name?"

The waitress darted out the front door. "There was a telephone booth right in front of the restaurant," Lillian recalls, "and my brother, Ulysses, who was 16 years old, was standing next to the phone booth waiting on the bus to come home because he worked at the YMCA." Surmising that his big sister was at it again, Ulysses looked on with anticipation as the flummoxed waitress called the cops, warning that there was about to be a "race riot."

The rioters stood outside in calm solidarity, three resolute women, two white, one black. Chief Morken arrived on the double, interviewed the witnesses and opined that a diminutive black lady ought to be able to have a piece of pie with her friends in Bremerton. He arranged a meeting the next day with the president of the NAACP, the pastor of Ebenezer A.M.E. Church and the café owner, who decided to remove his "We serve whites only" sign. Lillian Walker and her growing circle of friends and admirers had done some more "educating."

A statewide struggle

The Bremerton branch of the NAACP played a leading role in a statewide struggle that took another 25 years to achieve lasting victories. From dime stores and bus stations, soda fountains and barber shops during the war years, the state's civil rights pioneers moved to the halls of the state Capitol in Olympia to press their case for equal rights. Forging coalitions with progressive unions, ministerial associations and service clubs, they formed "Civic Unity" and "Civic Society" committees. James Walker was the second president of the Bremerton branch of the NAACP; Lillian was the secretary. She well remembers addressing 500 postcards every month and going door to door to recruit new members and urge people to register to vote. Lillian went on to become state secretary of the NAACP and one of Kitsap County's most stalwart Democrats. The Walkers were both active in the push for a Fair Employment Practices Act, which was enacted by the Legislature in 1949.

Bremerton schools were a bright spot in the civil rights picture. While there were few black teachers in the 1940s when the Walkers arrived, the staff and administrators were generally progressive. Mrs. Walker remembers only one incident. Ulysses arrived from Illinois in 1943 to live with his sister and brother-in-law. Soon thereafter he came home from school uncharacteristically glum. Lillian knew something was wrong. His teacher had used racial epithets in the classroom. The next morning, Lillian marched down to the school, took the woman aside and warned, "If it happens again, I'll have your job. I know your boss doesn't believe in that." Chastened, the teacher said, "Yes, Mrs. Walker."

Lillian in action was something to behold. Soon after they arrived in Bremerton James needed a haircut so they stopped at a shop not far from the shipyard. The barber, who was white, told James, "Well, if you come back after 5 o'clock, we'll close the shades and I'll cut your hair." Lillian was outraged. "If he couldn't cut a black man's hair in bright daylight, there was no way we were going to go there. So I said to James, 'Excuse me, honey, you will not be back after 5 o'clock. We will not go anyplace that the shade is closed. If you're going to cut his hair, you'll cut it right now, because if you don't cut it, I will cut it when I get home because I *am* a barber.' " That was another thing Lillian had learned in her spare time back in Carrier Mills. From then on, she cut James' hair, James Jr.'s hair and her brothers' hair. Lewis Allen had also moved from Illinois to Bremerton and landed a job at the shipyard.

On May 3, 1943, the Walkers moved into the house where Lillian still lives. The price was $3,300, and they endured a lot of rigmarole about insurance and the down payment. The banker's name, ironically, was Walker. Finally, a white real estate man offered to loan them the down payment. "Do you know what you're doing?" said the banker. "Yes," said the real estate man. "I trust Mr. and Mrs. Walker. They said they'd pay me and I believe them." He was a "very kindly white man," Mrs. Walker recalls. "People were impressed by our attitude. And we paid him back, every month, right on time."

After the war

Boeing B-29's dropped history's first A-bomb on Hiroshima on August 6, 1945, and reduced Nagasaki to radioactive rubble three days later. V-J Day came on Aug. 14. *The Bremerton Sun's* front page featured that good news and the bad news that $6 billion worth of Navy contracts had been canceled. There was a mass exodus of blacks, 22,000 workers in all. Blacks who stayed found themselves foreclosed from certain jobs and saw their wages lag behind whites. The Walkers had too much emotional equity in Bremerton, too many friends, to pick up and leave. Besides, James was moving up at work. The NAACP lost members, but it was still energetic. Some blacks who were to play key roles in the years to come returned from the war to reclaim their jobs at the Navy Yard. One was Al Colvin, a

VJ Day crowds in front of Forget-Me-Not Florists and Olberg Drugs at Pacific and 4th Street in Bremerton on August 14, 1945. Confetti flutters from the third floor windows. *Puget Sound Naval Shipyard*

member of the famed World War II black fighter squadron, the Tuskegee Airmen. The Colvins and Walkers quickly became good friends.

It was in 1947 that Dorothy "Dotsy" Fine, one of Lillian's PTA pals, recruited her to a campaign to form a YWCA in Bremerton. Lillian and her bosom buddy, Marie Greer, were among 20 women who volunteered to be board members. Before long, working with the Missionary Society of the church and the PTA, distributing handbills and using word of mouth, they had networked their way to 1,600 members. The YWCA opened with a lounge and a hot plate in 1948. "Coffee was 5 cents a cup, if you could afford it—and if you couldn't afford it, you got it anyway," Lillian recalls. The YWCA in Bremerton was built on bake sales, rummage sales, a grant here and a grant there. It became a crucial part of the social services fabric of the community, offering classes in everything from sewing and cooking to dance and self-defense. Young women had opportunities to grow and learn and have wholesome recreation and socializing.

Blacks in Washington saw some of their own finally find places in the corridors of power. In 1950, the Walkers' friend, civil rights attorney Charles M. Stokes, became the first black state legislator in the history of King County. A staunch Republican, Stokes championed the Civil Rights Omnibus Bill, one of the most progressive civil rights measures in the nation. He went on to become King County's first black district court judge. "He was flamboyant, articulate and brilliant and just an outstanding lawyer and a wonderful human being," says Charles Z. Smith, who in 1988 became the first ethnic minority on the Washington Supreme Court. A former King County deputy prosecutor and Superior Court judge, Smith knew Stokes well.

Black activists in Bremerton and Seattle were close allies. In addition to the Urban League and the NAACP, Seattle had an activist chapter of the Civil Rights Congress. The Walkers attended those events whenever they could.

By the end of the war, most of the whites-only signs in Bremerton had come down, although an undercurrent of racism remained. The U.S.

Supreme Court's landmark 1954 decision on school desegregation galvanized the modern civil rights movement. Everywhere in America blacks were still fighting for equal opportunity two centuries after the right to rise had been declared self-evident. As a boy, Lincoln memorized a history of the United States by an Irish immigrant named William Grimshaw, who noted with surprise and regret that the "colonists turned a blind eye to slavery despite lofty words." Grimshaw asserted, "Let us not only declare by words but demonstrate by our actions that 'all men are created equal.'"

Judge Charles Moorehead Stokes, a Northwest civil rights pioneer, in the 1950s.

All that was lost on the Bremerton drug store owner who on September 18, 1954, refused to let James Walker buy a cup of coffee at his soda fountain. "I didn't serve niggers in Texas," he declared, "and I'll go to hell before I serve them here." To hell you say? The Bremerton branch of the NAACP was pleased to oblige. There was a grade school about a block away from the drug store. "The little colored kids if they went down and got an ice cream cone had to stay outside, no matter what the weather was. But the little white kids could sit at the counter. *This is wrong!*" Mrs. Walker declares, scooting forward in her chair and swiping the air.

After a strategy session and a call to Philip Burton, another revered Seattle civil rights attorney, James Walker and his friend Whittier Johnson volunteered to throw down the gauntlet. The drug store owner "didn't know he was set up because we had white and black witnesses" there when he refused to serve the two men, Lillian recalls. Burton immediately filed a Kitsap County Superior Court complaint asserting that James Walker's civil rights had been violated. "We got telephone calls at 2 and 3 o'clock in the morning, threatening us, saying what they were going to do if we didn't drop the case," Mrs. Walker recalls. "They'd say, 'We know you're in there! You

Rosa Parks, who in 1955 refused to surrender her seat to a white passenger on a bus in Montgomery, Alabama, ushering in the modern civil rights movement. The Rev. Martin Luther King Jr. is in the background. *National Archives.*

niggers had better come out!' " White neighbors vowed to protect them.

The druggist settled out of court with the Walkers and grudgingly agreed to cease discrimination. It was one more seemingly small step on the road to equality. A larger one took place 2,100 miles away the next year when Rosa Parks wouldn't go to the back of the bus. She was arrested and young Martin Luther King Jr. helped organize a citywide bus boycott by blacks. James and Lillian Walker watched the newsreels and knew they were now part of something much bigger than Bremerton.

Decent housing was a major sticking point. In Washington State the push to remove the covenants that denied minorities equal access to housing began in the late 1940s and finally came to pass in the 1960s when the movement was at its zenith. State Rep. Sam Smith, a charismatic black Democrat who had defeated Stokes in 1958, forged a bipartisan coalition to "see the light" and pass a state open housing law in 1967. De facto housing segregation via "gentlemen's agreements" and "redlining" existed in Bremerton well into the 1960s, according to the Walkers. In the mid-1950s, when the Walkers had two young children—Jimmy, born in 1945, and June five years later—they went looking for a bigger house. The real estate man tried to steer them to Navy Yard City along Sinclair Inlet where many black families lived. Lillian had already spotted a nice house in another neighborhood. It had a for sale sign in the front yard. She called the Realtor and told him all about it. "Well, that's $28,000," he replied condescendingly. That was way beyond their means, but Lillian shot back, "I don't remember that we gave you a price that we couldn't meet." He never called back, so she called another real estate agency, made an appointment to see the house and asked two white friends, Marie and Jim Morris, to go along. The real estate man got out of the car, strolled up to Marie and said, "Hi, Mrs. Walker." Marie said, "*I'm the maid.* This is Mrs. Walker." Lillian loved watching him squirm. James could barely contain himself. "The guy hem-hawed. I bet he made five trips, up and back, up and back, to the house." Finally, he showed them the house, which was lovely. After the tour, Lillian nonchalantly advised, "We'll let you know whether we want it or not."

"We felt that we were moving forward," she says of the post-war years. "At least we had moved off of the (whites-only) signs. But there were other issues. The paper would not print a Negro's picture on the front page unless he had committed some terrible crime, like raping a woman or killing someone." In the 1950s, according to Mrs. Walker and other longtime black residents of Bremerton, things changed at *The Sun*, thanks to reporters Gene Gisley and Adele Ferguson. Gisley, who died in 2007,

James and Lillian with their son, James Walker Jr., mid-1940s.

had an open-door policy to the public when he became *The Sun's* editor in 1969. "He was *really* a good guy," Mrs. Walker says. "If we went down to the paper, we could either talk to him or Adele, and we knew we were going to get what we wanted," which was "to be treated like everyone else in Bremerton." Ferguson, who arrived around the same time as the Walkers in the early 1940s and became the widest-read political columnist in the state, says Lillian has always been a livewire and "the black people in Bremerton were first-rate folks."

Education is her mantra

Lillian and James had part-time janitorial jobs at a bank as well as the theater. They also took classes at Olympic College, he in electronics, she in bookkeeping, typing and shorthand. By the time he retired after 38 years with the federal government, James had parlayed his appetite for learning, his efficiency and affability into a post as assistant office manager for the Defense Contract Administrative Service in Seattle. "I always encourage everyone to get as much education as they possibly can," Lillian says. "That is something no one can ever take away from you." In the early 1950s, James was also the part-time Bremerton-area business manager for *The Northwest Enterprise*, a black newspaper based in Seattle. Lillian helped him with the billing and distribution and held several office jobs over the years. She was a bookkeeper for a real estate company in Tacoma and for the Kitsap Community Action Program. James was a Mason; Lillian was in Eastern Star. When they began raising Jimmy and June, they immersed themselves in the PTA, Campfire Girls, Cub Scouts, Boy Scouts and their church—Ebenezer African Methodist Episcopal, which they joined in 1941, shortly after arriving in Bremerton. Asked what sort of church work she has done over the past 68 years, Lillian chuckles and says, "The missionary women of the church went to a meeting in Seattle one day, and they asked me, 'Well, what office have you held in the church?' I said, 'I've been everything but the minister!' I was trustee. I was a steward. I was the secretary of the Sunday School. I've been on the Trustees' Board, and I've been on the Steward Board, and I've been the president of the Missionary Society." She was also a founder and president of Church Women United. "I want to make it clear," she says, "that when we arrived I met a lot of white people who weren't racist—especially the women who I helped start the Church Women United. That was women from every church, black and white. At one time we had about 150 members. ...You know, I tell people, I have as many white friends as I have black friends."

Lillian with her family Bible.
John Hughes for The Legacy Project

Among the kids who attended Ebenezer, Mrs. Walker was a legend in her own time as the decorum enforcer. "When we were young, we were afraid of her," says Althea Colvin, whose parents, Al and Hazel, were good friends of the Walkers. "If anybody acted up in church, Mrs. Walker—she didn't care whose child it was; she didn't have to know you—she would pick the child up and take it outside. I don't know what she did, but when they came back in that child wouldn't say a word! All the kids who went to church there, they respected Mrs. Walker. She could just look at you."

In the 1980s, Al Colvin became Bremerton's first black City Council member. He was already one of Kitsap County's most respected citizens. It was a different town in 1946 when he returned from the war and sent a plane ticket to his teenage sweetheart in Alabama. Hazel Colvin recalls being surprised to encounter overt discrimination in Bremerton. She thought she'd left that behind. Pregnant and feeling unwell, she went to the same drug store where James Walker had been refused service. She just wanted a cool drink, but "sat there and sat there" as the waitresses ignored her.

There were many speed bumps—and detours—on the road to equality in Bremerton and from sea to shining sea. But Althea Colvin, who graduated from high school in Bremerton in 1966, says she never experienced racial prejudice in girlhood—the legacy of the Walkers, her parents and the other civil rights pioneers in Kitsap County, black and white. Hazel Colvin marvels at Lillian's constancy. "Lillian Walker is the same person today as the person I met in the 1940s—always a real energetic person. She and James have been the most wonderful friends." Althea seconds the motion: "Over the years, she's been the most loving, humble caring person and whenever I see her, she just loves to see me. She calls Mom all the time to see that she's OK."

Mrs. Walker, who seems to be everywhere at once, was treasurer of the Bremerton Garden Club and has been active in the Kitsap County Democratic Party since the 1940s, serving as a precinct committeewoman in the 1970s. She was a member of the board of the Carver Civic Club, founded in 1948 as the Bremerton affiliate of the National Association of Colored Women's Clubs. The association dates back to 1896, "a time when Negro women were seen as chattel," Lillian notes. The club disbanded as its members aged, but Mrs. Walker is helping City Councilwoman Dianne Robinson revive it. They now have 14 members. "I just watch Mrs. Walker and try to follow her lead," Robinson says. "She knows parliamentary procedure like you wouldn't believe."

Helping to found the YWCA of Kitsap County is one of Lillian's proudest achievements, and its role has expanded. In the 1970s, two staff members at Olympic College had an idea for a shelter for women and children who were victims of domestic violence. They formed a partnership with the YWCA. "ALIVE"—Alternatives to Living In a Violent Environment—was born. It was controversial at first. Some said that wasn't part of the YWCA's core mission. Lillian wasn't buying that. Too many women "just had nowhere to go" to piece their lives back together, she said. Others endured abuse in silence because they were afraid and had no one to tell. Her own

At a state meeting in Seattle in 1959, members of the Carver Civic Club of Bremerton, their spouses and children pose for a picture. From left: Sarah Jones, Lillian Walker, Marie Greer, James Walker, Gertrude Joseph, Gladys Hill, June Walker (front), David Joseph, Lillian Wilson (back), Alyce Eagans, Elwood Greer and Hazel Colvin. The club was founded in 1948 as the Bremerton affiliate of the National Association of Colored Women's Clubs. In 2010, Lillian Walker received the Mary Church Terrell Lifetime Achievement Award from the National Association.

father had a temper that could turn abusive, and her mother—remember, she had suffered brain damage at the hands of her stepfather—"just took it." Mrs. Walker recalls, "When James and I were getting married I said, 'I need to tell you something: If you ever hit me, you better knock me out. Make sure I'm out cold, and be gone when I come to.'" James said, "Honey, I wouldn't hit you! I love you." Lillian said, "I know. I thought my dad loved my mother. But I'm telling you, I *will* not take a beating off of anybody."

Lillian Walker and her sisters in arms "raised the bar for women's involvement in Kitsap County," Linda Joyce, the executive director of the YWCA, said at a 60th anniversary celebration in 2008. Congressman Norm Dicks, a Bremerton native, was there, too, to salute one of his biggest fans. "Lillian has been one of the pillars of our community," Dicks said, "someone we all respect so much. It's great to see her get the recognition she has long deserved....The YWCA has done such a good job in eliminating racial barriers and supporting diversity in our community....And domestic violence, this is a subject that in our lifetimes, Lillian, wasn't even talked about!" Mrs. Walker's eyes filled with tears as she received a standing ovation. "You have qualities," she told the crowd. "I have qualities; we need to bring people together for the best of the community. That's the way I work on anything I work on. If it's going to better you, it's going to better me. The Golden Rule has always been my motto." Linda Joyce noted, "She's been there at every twist and turn. Marie Greer has passed away so Mrs. Walker is now our only surviving charter member. She reminds us of the commitment and vision of the ladies who were the backbone of this organization."

Mrs. Walker and Mrs. Greer, who died in 2008 at the age of 94, were two peas in a pod—active in the NAACP, the YWCA, the Carver Civic Club and Ebenezer A.M.E. Church. They became even closer after they lost their husbands. "They went everywhere together, did everything together and even dressed alike," Councilwoman Robinson says. "I called them 'The Gold Dust Twins.'"

Lillian and Marie met in the fall of 1941 when she and James joined

From left: Alyce Eagans, Hazel Colvin, Dianne Robinson, and Lillian Walker at the Kitsap County Historical Society Museum's presentation on "Segregation and Civil Rights in Kitsap County" in 2009. Carolyn J. Yaschur, © *Kitsap Sun*

Ebenezer. In 1943, they helped organize Unit No. 1134 of the NAACP. Mrs. Walker is now the sole surviving charter member. Her brother, Lewis Allen, was chairman of the Fair Housing Act program for the NAACP and served as president of the branch in the 1950s. Loxie Eagans, its 10th president in the 1960s, was deputy Equal Employment Opportunity officer for the shipyard and a vigorous civic leader. Over the years, the branch has hosted a number of prestigious visitors, including Roy Wilkins, national director of the NAACP. It staged a march in the 1960s

Lillian with her best friend, Marie Greer.

in support of Dr. King's push for voting rights and an end to Jim Crow laws. In the 1970s it established a credit union that was Al Colvin's pride and joy. The branch also developed a strong partnership with Olympic College, launched scholarship programs and developed a nationally recognized Youth Chapter. It successfully lobbied Kitsap County to establish an Affirmative Action policy. In 1986, when the City of Bremerton balked at making Martin Luther King's birthday a holiday, the NAACP jawboned compliance, with its dynamic former president, Larry Greene, leading the charge. "We've come a long way in Bremerton," Mrs. Walker says, "but you can't stop fighting ignorance."

Bremerton Mayor Glenn Jarstad appointed Mrs. Walker to the Regional Library Board in 1972. She served for seven years, particularly proud to have played a key role in the design and construction of the new Sylvan Way Branch, which opened in 1978. She was board chairman at the time. Lillian and James were active in promoting senior citizen programs and served two terms apiece on the Kitsap County Area Agency on Aging Advisory Council. In 1997, Kitsap County's Martin Luther King Memorial

Congressman Norm Dicks presents Lillian with the YWCA 60th anniversary commemorative plaque in 2008. Lillian was the only living founding member. At right is Alyce Eagans. © *Kitsap Sun*

Scholarship Fund Committee named them "MLK Citizens of the Century" for producing a total of 100 years of service to the community and the nation. James said he was surprised because he didn't think the work they'd been doing "was such a big deal." Lillian added, "We knew we had a lot of friends, but getting this award for doing what we thought was right... well, I feel really honored."

Their son says it was largely unspoken but well understood that his parents had high expectations when it came to education. "I was always a person who wanted to push ahead," the epidemiologist says, "and I had my internal goals, but they recognized the importance of education and provided opportunities. ... Family and family life was always important to them." They were also "friendly, sociable people, and they tried to make friends with strangers and defuse any situations." Like Althea Colvin, James T. Walker Jr. feels he grew up "sheltered from some of uglier parts of life" because his parents and the other Kitsap County civil rights pioneers had already challenged "a lot of the institutional racism."

Alyce Eagans, who arrived in Bremerton in the 1940s right after she graduated from high school in Arkansas, joined the NAACP as a teenager and went on to become its president. Her future husband, Loxie, and the Walkers were role models. "James was very quiet—not nearly as talkative as Mrs. Walker!" she says. "But he had a great sense of humor and was a very effective leader. And Mrs. Walker was something else! She just didn't sit back. She made things happen. She's been a livewire all her life. Even today, she can think of more things than I can. Her brain is always working. She's just amazing!"

Lillian is "deeply humbled" by all the awards she has received in recent years, quipping that she has just "out-lived" most everyone else in the running. The PTA gave her its Golden Acorn. The YWCA gave her its Founder's Award and the Democrats presented her their Lifetime Achievement award. The NAACP calls her "a living treasure." She's running out of wall space for all those plaques. The 2009 Liberty Bell Award from the Kitsap County Bar Association is one of which she is particularly proud. Her friend Robin Hunt, a judge on the Washington Court of Appeals, nominated her, saying that Mrs. Walker has "contributed in countless ways to the effective functioning of our government and promoted better understanding of our Constitution, the Bill of Rights and the rule of law.

Lillian Walker with her Liberty Bell Award.

Linda Joyce, Executive Director of the Kitsap County YWCA, hugs Lillian Walker, a charter member, at a 2008 event to celebrate the Y's 60th anniversary. Carolyn J. Yaschur, © *Kitsap Sun*

Her courageous persistence to insist on equal rights has brought about change in our community....She is the living embodiment of Lincoln's Emancipation Proclamation and Martin Luther King's dream. And she has accomplished these goals without rancor, but rather with an attitude that others simply needed to be 'educated.'" Washington's young Attorney General, Rob McKenna, was awed by Mrs. Walker's eloquently humble acceptance speech as she received the Liberty Bell Award. He said it was the closest he would ever come to meeting Rosa Parks.

"This wonderful life"

With an assortment of aches and pains, Lillian Walker, closing in on 100, has her good days and bad days. But the good ones are lovely, especially when friends stop by, and the bad ones "not so bad." She says she knows she will be leaving Planet Earth for a better place "pretty soon" but she's thankful for "this wonderful life" she has lived. Oh how she misses James, who died at 89 in 2000. They were married for 59 years. "If I had searched the world over I couldn't have found a better mate." Sometimes it seems as if he's still here. "The other night I looked over (at his picture) and I could see him coming through the door. Or I go to bed and think, 'OK, honey, I got the bed warmed for you!' And he says, 'OK, put your cold foot up on my leg.' That's what I heard for all those years. Now I've got to put on socks."

Elwood and Marie Greer are gone, too, as are Loxie Eagans and Al

Colvin. But the memories are still so vivid, and she has younger friends like Alyce, Judge Hunt and Councilwoman Robinson. They adore her and check in often. Her daughter June in Tacoma is attentive, and James Jr. calls often. A young woman she has known from church interviewed her for a class at the college, which was gratifying. She worries about the kids today. Robinson, to their dismay, has a hard time getting younger people interested in the NAACP and black history. The Kitsap County Black Historical Society is a labor of love for the Bremerton councilwoman. What she has accomplished is "just terrific—collecting all those pictures and documents," Mrs. Walker says. "I just can't give that girl enough credit. If every kid—and not just black—in Bremerton, in Kitsap County, in Washington State, if they could read what she has done and really *listen* to what she's done, they'd have a lesson. I mean a *brilliant* lesson."

Robinson visits schools, trying to impress on young folks, especially minorities, that people like Mrs. Walker and Rosa Parks put their lives on the line to secure equal rights. "I'm just so proud to say she's my friend," Robinson says. "I worry every day about where the next Lillian Walker or Marie Greer or Loxie Eagans is going to come from. Mrs. Walker always

Lillian with Councilwoman Dianne Robinson. *John Hughes for The Legacy Project*

says, 'Who's gonna take over for us?' When you read the history of the things they did you're inspired. They made a real contribution to making this a better community. Growing up in Pensacola, Fla., the Community Center clubhouse taught me so many things," Robinson adds. "I learned how to dress; what clothes to wear; to crochet. I went to camp. I learned how to kill a snake! And I was connected to the older people in the community. There wasn't a day that I didn't go knock on some old person's door and say, 'Ma'am can I help you with anything today? You need your yard raked?' The childhood that I had growing up in a community and being involved and having role models like Mrs. Walker and Mrs. Greer was so important. Those two ladies were so alike. When I first got here, they said, 'Well what do you know about black history?' Then they saw what I was like and what I was going to do, and they said, 'Well, Dianne, that's very important.' I want to be able to tell these stories so that they're preserved and to show that people here in Kitsap County have made a big contribution, so that people can understand how things were and how they got changed."

Mrs. Walker listens and nods. *"This is right,"* she says. That's one of her favorite phrases. What advice does she have for her six grandchildren, three great-grandchildren and the rest of us? "Don't complain. If you've got something to complain about, well, work at it and make it better. And, treat everybody right. I don't care who or what they are, treat them right. You don't have the authority to mistreat anybody, because that's why we are here—to help each other. If you can help somebody, help them." And if she could go on TV and talk to the minority kids who often seem to take for granted the freedoms she fought for? "I'd try to tell them, 'You don't know what you're doing. ...Know your history! We have fought for you to have the rights to go in and sit down and eat, to go and apply for a job.' And I'd tell them you don't go around with your pants hanging down your behind! You don't do that and get ahead."

For the record, Lillian had that advice months before an AARP-age rapper crashed the "American Idol" auditions in 2010 and had America chanting, "Pants on the ground. Pants on the ground. Lookin' like a fool with your pants on the ground!" She's always been ahead of her time.

Oral History

Research by John C. Hughes, Lori Larson,
Dianne Robinson, Robin Hunt, James T. Walker Jr.,
Carolyn Neal, Charleen Burnette, Dick Allen and Bob Johnson

Interviews by John C. Hughes, chief oral historian for The Legacy Project
Transcription by Lori Larson & John Hughes

Lillian Walker Interview 1
June 8, 2009

John C. Hughes: The Legacy Project is honored to be with Mrs. Lillian Walker at her home in Bremerton. Judge Robin Hunt, who first told us about Mrs. Walker, is with us as well. Mrs. Walker is a pioneer in the Civil Rights movement in Kitsap County and a charter member of the NAACP and YWCA in Bremerton, as well as a former postmaster of the Sinclair Park Branch Post Office. She's seen some really remarkable changes in American society in her wonderfully long and eventful life. It's such a privilege, Mrs. Walker. When Judge Hunt called me and told me about you I was really excited. My mom—how I wish she was still alive—was born in the same year you were.

Lillian Walker: Oh really? 1913.

Hughes: 1913. And she grew up in Oklahoma and went to college at Northwestern in Chicago as a young woman. She was a good Baptist and she *hated* prejudice of any kind. And she had some white girlfriends in Chicago who were really nasty to her because she had black chums as well.

She was your kind of woman.

Walker: Bless her heart. You know, I tell people, I have as many white friends as I have black friends. I've tried to treat people like I want to be treated.

Hughes: The Golden Rule.

Walker: That's right. "Do you unto others as you would have them do unto you." I don't think you can go wrong. Now, I've run across some people that have wanted to fight. I've had my share of fights. I fought in school. I didn't do much fighting in high school because I had to walk three and a half miles so I wasn't fighting anything. In grade school, we had a big yard where at recess we'd play ball or whatever. But there wasn't a boy in that school up to the eighth grade that dare tackle me because I'd beat him because I was raised with brothers and we rassled. No boy my age or even a little older would dare say something nasty to me.

Hughes: I wish more Caucasian people had the experience that I've had. And that is to see prejudice first hand, because my children, who were adopted from Korea, were subjected to some racism at school. Nothing hurts you more, I think, than to be a parent and to have a child come home and say, "They called me a 'gook,' or a 'chink.' Or some ugly name.

Walker: I've been there. We went back to Illinois to my home and my husband's home. And my brother, he was 16 years younger than I was. And he wanted to come home (to Bremerton) with us for a year….And mom and dad said, "Well, if you send him back at the end of the year." "OK." So we brought him and he went to school in sixth grade. One day he came home from school and he just wasn't the same. I said, "What's the matter?" And he didn't say much. I said, "Ulysses, what is wrong? What happened?" So he told me his teacher had read something derogatory and used the word "nigger" in class, then had him read something that went along the same lines, and it hurt him. To look at him you couldn't tell whether he was a Negro or a white boy. But anyway, that's beside the point. So the next morning I went down to his school and I asked for his teacher. I said, "I don't like what you did yesterday to my brother. But I can tell you this: If you do it again I'll have your job." I said, "Your boss is not like that. He doesn't believe in that, and I bet he doesn't know what you've done. I'm sure he does not approve of what you did. But you do it again and he will know it from me. And I'll have your job." It never happened again.

Hughes: What did she say? Was she chagrined?

Walker: She was. I don't believe the lady had ever been confronted, on anything.

Hughes: What year?

Walker: That was '43.

Hughes: 1943. That was a good year. That was the year I was born. I'm almost exactly 30 years younger than you are.

Walker: Oh really? Bless your heart. You've got a lot more ahead of you.

Hughes: I hope so.

Walker: Take it one day at a time.

Hughes: To quote my mother, "I hope I'm doing better than just being upright and taking nourishment."

Walker: (laughing)

Hughes: Well, what I want to do is start at the beginning.

Walker: You mean when I was born? I was born 10-2-1913, at 4:30 in the morning. My parents were Moses and Hazel Allen.

Hughes: Were you born at home?

Walker: Yes, in 1913, we lived near Carrier Mills, Illinois. There's a little town there. It's not like Bremerton, but they had stores that you could go in and buy clothes or whatever. It was a country town. It's called the Lakeview community. I was born out in the country about three and a half miles from town. When you leave town there was a service station on this side road and then there was a farmhouse there. Then the next mile or two there's a farmhouse. And then you go on down the road and you up the hill and there's another farmhouse there and one here. Then you go another two or three miles and there's another.

Hughes: It's rural!

Walker: Yes, it's *really* rural.

EDITOR'S NOTE: Carrier Mills has lost some 1,100 residents since the population peak of 2,943 in 1920. Free blacks founded the early pioneer settlement of Lakeview, a mile south of Carrier Mills, shortly after the War of 1812. The History of Saline County (published by the Saline County Genealogical Society in 1997) states that "Lakeview, a colored community south of town (Carrier Mills), is an older settlement than Carrier Mills. It is the oldest black settlement in Illinois. It was first named Pond Settlement because of the swamp land that surrounded it. According to local tradition free blacks living in the Pond Settlement helped runaway slaves and indentured servants escape from the saline works and the Old Slave House near Equality, Illinois. In 1850, a Union Church was established near Carrier Mills in Saline Co., Illinois. Most members were either Baptist or Methodist. An African Methodist Episcopal Church was organized at the home of Irvin Allen, who built a one-room log church building on his property. After the church burned, the congregation rebuilt and moved the church to Carrier Mills, where it sits today....After the closure of the Lakeview School in the 1950s, many people moved to the east side of Carrier Mills. There was much tension felt between the white and black populations in the town."

Hughes: How far were you from any big city, from Chicago?

Walker: Well, from Chicago about 350 miles. Harrisburg, the township, was about 12 miles from our farm. And mind you now, we had horses and wagons, horses and buggy. Sometimes my dad would drive the team to Harrisburg. Mom and Dad had a small farm. And on Friday they would pick vegetables, beans, peas, potatoes, whatever. And then he would take these to Harrisburg where there was a coal mine, what did they call it?—A "number three." That's where there was a miners' house. So he came back

The Allen family home near Carrier Mills, Illinois, in the 1930s. Standing at left, wearing a hat, is Lillian's father, Moses; in the middle wearing an apron is her mother, Hazel. Lillian is second from right. Her brother Lewis is reaching down to lift a child. Note that someone has been cut out of the photo. It was a boyfriend Lillian discovered had been two-timing her, "So, I cut him right out of the picture and scratched his name off the back. I couldn't stand to look at him anymore!"

home one Saturday evening and he hadn't sold anything. Mom said, "What happened?" And he said, "People don't have any money." That's when the Depression hit. So we had to can that stuff or eat it. But that was the first time that I realized (there was a Depression in America). We didn't realize we were poor. Like if we had to have cornbread on Saturday morning or any morning, and we were used to having biscuits, hot biscuits, we didn't want that cornbread. But that's what we got that one weekend because Dad forgot to take wheat to town to get a bag of flour. Now that to me spelled poor.

Hughes: So, who attended your birth? Would it have been a midwife?

Walker: A midwife, yes. I think she was the one that helped bring me into the world—either that or my grandmother. I'm not sure which. I don't remember that far back! (laughing)

Hughes: So, what was the birth order there? Were you the first of the children?

Walker: No. I was the third. My mother had a child before she and my dad married. That was my brother Shirley. And then they had a girl, Mary. I think she got in a fire or something. She and Shirley were playing in the fireplace. I don't know all the details. So there was Shirley, Mary, and then me, and then my brother, Lewis, who moved out here after we did. My mother had a total of 11 children (six of whom died young)....I was so excited to have a little sister, Juanita, but she lived only a few hours.... Lord knows, life was hard. Think of my poor mother.

Hughes: For the record, Lillian Allen Walker has no middle name?

Walker: No. Well, when I was born my mom and dad named me Arlena Lillian Bianna Allen. Now where they got this name, I don't know. But I was teased and made fun of, so when I came out here I (got the county officials back in Illinois) to change my name to just Lillian Allen Walker.

Hughes: But nobody ever called you by those other names, did they?

Walker: The kids at school did. They made fun of it. They'd go, "Oh, there's Arlena!"

Hughes: It was kind of a mouthful.

Walker: Well, it was, and they made fun of it. So I just hated it!

Hughes: Did your folks call you Lillian or something else?

Walker: They called me Lillian or "Sis."

Hughes: Did you know your grandparents? Were they living in that same community?

Walker: My dad's father and mother (were there). I remember my Grandmother Elvira. When I was about 6 she gave me my first rag doll. She made me a rag doll. She died shortly after. I don't remember her death. But they tell me that one day she came home and she went in and took a bath, put on her dress clothes, and they asked her, "Elvira, what's going on?" "Well, I'm gonna die." She laid down on the bed and *died*.

Hughes: My gosh, she had this amazing premonition.

Walker: That's right.

Hughes: I understand from something your son James gave me that the oral tradition in the family is that Grandma Elvira was the offspring of a "Portuguese" man. From my own research, I'm sure he was a colored man. And her mother was the white daughter of a plantation owner.

Walker: That's it. Grandma Elvira's mother was the white daughter of a slave master.

Hughes: And they fled from Tennessee to Illinois because the plantation owner had fallen on dire straits financially and might sell off their children?

Walker: That's the story we've heard.

Hughes: And Grandfather Allen?

Walker: Willis Allen. He was still alive when I was a child. I think I was around 11 or 12, something like that, when he passed. He was living with us. He was sitting out on the front porch. And us kids, that was one our jobs in the summertime was to keep the flies off of grandpa.

Lillian Walker's aunt's children in the 1890s.

And one day, one of us came in and told Dad, "There's something's wrong with grandpa!" Something happened to him and they took him in and got him on the bed. And the doctor finally came. Evidently he'd had a stroke because I think he lasted about three days and then he was gone.

Hughes: Could you call the doctor in a rural area like that in those days?

Walker: You call the doctor and he might get there in three days, or something like that, because he was in Harrisburg.

Hughes: And Harrisburg was how far?

Walker: About 12 miles, and we had no phone. So that meant we had to either go to town (or find someone who could call). I don't think the neighbor had a phone at that point. One of my brothers that was younger than me—Charles—was 2 or 3 years old when he woke up choking. He was having some kind of an attack. I woke mom and dad up and we worked with him. They put a spoon in his mouth. And somebody went to get the doctor. Well, the boy was dead when the doctor got there.

Hughes: Times were tough, weren't they?

Walker: *Oh boy*, you aren't kidding. If we had a toothache, and if it had a hollow in it, Dad would either put a piece of carbide, you know what the coal miners used, in it. Or pull it because we couldn't afford a dentist.

Hughes: I never heard of putting carbide in there to fill it.

Walker: That's what happened in our time. See, you weren't born yet.

Hughes: Just to be clear, we've been talking about your paternal grandparents, your father's parents?

Walker: Yes. Willis and Elvira Allen.

Hughes: Please tell us your mother's maiden name and more about her.

Walker: My mother's maiden name was Williams, Hazel Ethel Williams. Her mother lived in town. Her name was Mary Eddings. Mother's stepdad was Warren Eddings. And some weekends maybe all of us would go to town and spend the weekend, or Saturday night, with grandma. And then we'd go to church with her. She went to a Methodist Church there in Carrier Mills. Now in the country we went to a Baptist Church and then we had a Holy Sanctified Church. But we belonged to the Baptist Church. The church was about a mile from our house and then you had another two miles to go to town.

Hughes: Define a "Sanctified" Church for me please, Mrs. Walker. Is that a Pentecostal kind of church?

Walker: Well, it's on that order. But they believe in shouting; not that the Methodist Church or the Baptist Church don't. They were a local church. I think they had a minister. But they had a lot of singing and a lot of shouting. Like, oh a few summers ago, our church (here in Bremerton) had some of that and I said, "Lord, we are turning into Ebenezer Holy Sanctified Church!"…And some of them, they're hollering and shouting, or they call it shouting, so much that you can't understand what the preacher's saying. And it kind of irked me, but I tried not to show it. I guess I'm spoiled because since I broke my hip some Sundays I couldn't get to church unless I had a ride or something. And sometimes I wake up sick and I just can't get there. But there have been some changes at church…

Moses and Hazel Allen.

(Bremerton City Council member Dianne Robinson, an expert on the history of blacks in Kitsap County, arrives to listen in.)

Hughes: (addressing Robinson) You have done amazing work. The historical stuff you have preserved for your community is really important, Dianne.

Walker: She has really done it! I just can't give that girl enough credit. If every kid—and not just black—in Bremerton, in Kitsap County, in Washington State, if they could read what she has done and really *listen* to what she's done, they'd have a lesson. I mean a *brilliant* lesson.

Hughes: Like you said earlier—you better "know your history."

Walker: There you go. Right, right. I tell you, she can't get enough credit for what she has done.

Hughes: Mrs. Walker is talking about churches she went to, Dianne. So, mostly you went to the Baptist Church?

Walker: Yes.

Hughes: Because it was closest?

Walker: Yes. It was the only church—well, that and that Holy Sanctified Church.

Hughes: Would these churches have been mostly people of color? Were they black folks?

Walker: Well, they were "black" in the term used now, but back then most of them were my color (lighter-skinned). And some of them were lighter. We wouldn't call them "Negroes." They were "colored" people. But some of them you didn't know what they were—a lot of them. Like my grandmother, my dad's mother.

Hughes: Did you love it when someone was commenting on President Obama's race and the president of Italy said, "I don't know what the big deal is. It just looks to me as if he has a beautiful suntan"?

Walker: That's really nice!

Hughes: I've got a picture of your parents (shows photo). I love this picture.

Walker: Yes, that's Mom and Dad.

Hughes: In the 1920 Census they're listed in this classic catch-all as "mulattoes." How would you define them?

Walker: Her mother was white and his mother was white, or so I've been told. His mother was from Tennessee and I don't know how she got to Carrier Mills. I had a cousin who knew all this but he died before I got to interview him. I think the story James told you about the slave master has the ring of truth to it.

Hughes: They say if you do your genealogy you'd better be prepared for what you find. You could find horse thieves and…

Walker: You aren't kidding!

Hughes: There's been a lot of genealogy done in my father's family. They're from Tennessee by way of Virginia.

Walker: You know I've met so many people from Tennessee and sometimes I feel like going up and asking them, "Was anybody in your family named Elvira?" because that was my grandma's name. (Examining another photo) The old lady here in this picture is Elvira Allen, my dad's mother.

Hughes: And who is this? (Pointing to a young woman with Grandma Elvira Allen) She's beautiful.

Walker: I don't know who she is. I think she's a daughter-in-law.

Hughes: One of the things that has always seemed so stupid to me about prejudice is that, first, it's self evident that we're all God's children and if you pull back the cuticle you're going to find a lot of mixed race in families.

Walker: You better believe it.

Hughes: And particularly in that era when people were owning other human beings—and sleeping with them. There are people in my family tree who look darker than your mom and dad. In the old saying of that era, it looks to me as if your parents "could have passed" (for white).

Walker: Well, they did because sometimes people thought they were white. When mom and dad would go to town to buy groceries or whatever. And then there was a family that lived along the way, Henry and Nora Cole, and they were brown skinned. And dad would stop to speak to them. They'd be outside or something and they'd say, "Oh, I thought you were a couple of old white people." And Dad would say, "No, this is Mo and Hazel."

Moses Allen, Lillian's father, as a young man.

Hughes: (laughing) That's great!

Walker: But we got that a lot.

Hughes: Was there prejudice in that community? Was there clearly a pecking order between people who were different shades of black and the white folks?

Walker: The pecking order would be if you were a "rat" or a "nigger"— a bad person no matter your color. When the word "nigger" comes up, I say, "What color are you?" People say, "What do you mean?" And I say, "You don't have to be black to be a 'nigger.' They're in every race, color, creed." You know, and it's *true*....But if you were living what we'd call the Christian life, and treating people like you wanted to be treated, then no matter what color you were you were accepted.

Hughes: So how many people of color would there have been in that area? Was Carrier Mills a town, or is it just sort of a wide spot in the road?

Walker: Carrier Mills is the town and then there's the Lakeview community. That's where a lot of these (black and mixed-race) families lived. I never did know whether Uncle Joe's wife was white or black because she looked like my grandmother. There were probably 600 or so colored people.

Hughes: You say your cousin who knew a lot of this history has passed on. Were you able to ever authenticate the slave roots (of the family)?

Walker: He said he had papers to prove where Grandma Elvira came from. But I never did get to read them because he lived in Michigan. And he came out here once and he said, "I should have brought that with me." But he didn't. And I don't know whether his son who lives in Michigan now, Harry, (has the information). I hear from him. We exchange e-mails all the time.

Hughes: I am blown away, as they say today, by the fact that you're nearly 96 years old and you're on the Internet doing all this stuff.

Walker: You know, I was on the ferry one day coming from Seattle. And a lady sat by me and she had her laptop. And I said, "That's interesting." And she said, "Do you have a computer?" I said, "I'm a computer illiterate. But, yes, I have one." She said, "Do you send e-mail and receive e-mail?" I said, "Yes." She said, "You're not illiterate then."

Hughes: Hardly.

Walker: There's a lot that I can't do. But there are some things I can do. When my son was taking his youngest daughter to different colleges out of high school to see which one she was going to pick, well, he would call me, "Mom, we're going to…" And he'd give me the e-mail. "Will you find out what their visiting hours are?" And I said, "Well, now, I can do that."

Hughes: I think it's pretty remarkable what you've done. There's a whole lot of people way younger than you are who can't find their way around the Internet, I'll tell you that. But let's go back to your roots: When you did your genealogy were you able to track relatives on both sides? Did they all arrive there in rural Illinois from the South?

Walker: Dad was born in Carrier Mills, and mom, I think she came from Springfield to Carrier Mills.

Hughes: Both of your parents, according the Census records, were born in Illinois.

Walker: Yes.

Hughes: And the grandparents, who lived just down the road, were they both from Tennessee?

Walker: I don't know. I think grandpa came from there. He told me that once because he lived with us for quite a while. When my brother and I were young we would come in and pretend we were roosters around him. You know how kids think because you're old you don't have good sense. And we'd come in and say, "We're Mr. and Mrs. so-and-so..."

Hughes: But that wasn't pulling anything over on him, was it?

Walker: Nooo, no! But we thought we were.

Hughes: How old was grandpa then?

Walker: He was elderly because we kids were eight or 10 years old when he lived with us. So he was in his sixties I'm sure. (Editor's note: The Census says Willis Allen was 70 in 1920 and born in Illinois, as was his father. His mother is listed as having been born in North Carolina.)

Hughes: There must be good longevity in this family of yours.

Walker: You know, when somebody asked me that—"Have you researched how many 95-year-old people there are in your family?"—I said, "Who am I going to research it on? There's nobody in my family that is past 91." My aunt, one of dad's sisters, she lived to be 91. But she was back there in Illinois, and I'm told she wasn't all there. What do they call it now? Alzheimer's. Anyway, she lost her mind.

Hughes: These pictures of your parents are absolutely classic. They look like people you'd really like to know. So dad was Moses, and his middle name was?

Walker: No middle name.

Hughes: And Hazel, your mom, her middle name?

Walker: Ethel.

Hughes: Tell me more about your parents. What was your dad like? What kind of man was he?

Walker: Well, how do I describe Dad? He worked in the coal mines part time. And he worked and raised the farm, and he had cows, horses, mules, pigs. And so his job was taking care of those. And mom would get up in the morning and—I remember one morning, I guess she hadn't had enough sleep or something. She laid down on the foot of the bed. And dad came up from taking care of the animals and he threw some water on her.

Hughes: Just to be playful you mean; just for fun?

Walker: To wake her up. "Ethel, get up!" Anyway, it made her angry but she got up and made breakfast. We had breakfast every day.

Hughes: What did she cook for breakfast?

Walker: Most of the time it was oatmeal and rice. It wasn't dry cereal. And if we wanted bacon and eggs we could have that. So we had a big breakfast every day. And we had a big lunch. One time when I was about nine years old, the day before we had picked green beans and I fixed those and was ready to cook them and she showed me how to cook them, what to put in the pot and everything. And then I was making cornbread for lunch, which we called "dinner." We had breakfast, dinner and supper. In the spring the eggs were small. So I was making cornbread and it didn't look quite right so I put two eggs in. Well, it was yellow. I put it in the slop barrel for the hogs. So dad and boys came home for dinner. "How come dinner isn't ready?" "Well, the bread is not quite done yet." And years later I told Mom what happened.

Hughes: What did your mother call your father?

Walker: She called him "Mose."

Hughes: And what did you call your parents?

Walker: Oh, "Mom" and "Dad."

Hughes: Was Dad a friendly, outgoing guy?

Walker: Yes. Some people that know me from there say, "You're just like your dad." Yeah. Some things that I do.

Hughes: These Census records can be really interesting, but sometimes they're hard to decipher. (Shows Mrs. Walker the Census records for 1920 and 1930).

Walker: I've never seen that.

Hughes: I'll make you copies. Early on there's always this part where it asks if you can read or write or if you've had any education. And in the 1920 Census it says that both of your parents could read and write. And then in 1930, it claims that your mother couldn't read or write.

Walker: Well, that's because when she was in the fourth grade her step-father hit her. They lived in town. When you went out the back door, there was a boardwalk and then at the end of that was a well. I think grandma was out there, and Mom was coming from there and he thought that Mom had told grandma something that she shouldn't have. So he hit her on the head and knocked her down. She never was able to read after that. They never sent her back to school.

Hughes: Could she have had some brain damage from being hit?

Walker: That's what we think. But they didn't take her to the doctor or anything. Later on she learned how to write her name. And she could count money because she kept track of her eggs and if somebody else was taking her eggs to town, she knew how much money she had coming back. She was sharp, but she just couldn't read print.

Hughes: What was her personality like?

Walker: Well, Mom was good at raising kids.

Hughes: Hard work!

Walker: You aren't kidding! And being the oldest girl, I had to help. Oh, getting back to that cornbread…

Hughes: Sure.

Walker: I'm not trying to confuse you.

Hughes: No, you're doing great! I got you off the cornbread story. It was *me*, not you!

Walker: Well, anyway, later on I told Mom what I'd done and she said, "Well, you threw away the best part of the cornbread." I said, "Now I know it, but I didn't know it then." I thought that I had put too much soda in it and made it yellow. It was just the eggs. So anyway when I got it done they ate it. Then for dinner we'd always have something light. We didn't have a big meal. Maybe leftovers or something like that.

Hughes: You're working hard during the day.

Walker: Right. Some people used to ask me, "Can you plough?" I don't know if you know the big double plough that you break ground with. I can use that. I don't think there was any implement on the farm that I couldn't use. I could run a hay rake. We didn't have anything that was electrical. It was all powered by muscle, horse pulling or something like that. I could use a double shovel and lay and rake corn on the Fourth of July. You had to work. You were part of the family and you had to work.

Hughes: What an incredible life you've had. You've seen rural America as it once was.

Walker: I've *lived* rural America.

Hughes: The Census says that in 1920 you were in Independence Township, the county is Saline, Illinois, and we've got Mose Allen, head of the family. It says that he's had some schooling and he was literate. He could read and write.

Walker: Yeah. He could.

Hughes: He's a coal miner, it says, and a farmer. It says they've got 15 acres. Does that make sense?

Walker: I thought it was 20 but maybe it was 15 acres.

Hughes: Like I say, they're often wrong on these reports. In 1920, it says Dad was 30 and Mom was 25. In 1930, it says he's 49 and she's 38.

Walker: She was born in 1886 and dad was born in 1880.

Hughes: Then the 1920 Census lists a son named Shirley. That's your *brother's* name?

Walker: Yeah, but I have a niece named Shirley, too.

Hughes: People forget that in the 1800s and early 1900s Shirley was a boy's name as well.

Walker: Yeah, when we moved from Carrier Mills to Stonefort, I went to a little country school and one of the boys there was named Shirley.

Hughes: Now, here on this 1920 Census report they've really mangled your name because it looks like "Lewialians"—"daughter." And then there's Lewis—a son.

Walker: Yes, Lewis.

Hughes: Then William, a son.

Walker: Yeah. But they really messed up my name. Since I've been out here I've tried to get my birth certificate. Well, they weren't issuing birth certificates.

Hughes: Sure, you're born at home. And they spelled your name "Lewialians."

Walker: That's what they sent me when I wrote to get my birth certificate. And I said, "You've got my name spelled wrong. My name is L-i-l-l-i-a-n."

Hughes: My mom was so angry over a similar thing. Her middle name was Fae and they misspelled it as Foe, F-o-e, on her birth certificate and that just irritated her no end. She said, "I'm not Mildred Foe!"…But back to the Census records: In 1930 it lists the Allens as Moses, Hazel, Lillian—they got it right this time—Lewis and Damon?

Walker: Yeah, I had a brother named Damon.

Hughes: And then there's your brother Ulysses, which they have spelled "Ulises." In 1930 Grandpa Willis Allen is missing. He must have passed on by then?

Walker: I think so. I'm sure he had.

Hughes: Now, wait a minute. Look at this: the acreage on your farm is listed as 20 in 1930. So, you're right. You're sharp as a tack, Mrs. Walker!… What was the atmosphere like at home? Was it close knit?

Walker: Oh yes. We've always been a close knit family. And in the evening we had what we call a library table in the living room and then we had the big potbelly stove. Dad would get up in the morning and clean out the stove, open both doors to let the fresh air in and build a fire. Then after it started getting warm then you could get up. He'd also start the fire in the kitchen stove, the big range, to get it ready for mom so she could cook breakfast. He'd get up at least an hour or an hour and a half before us.

Hughes: Like 5 a.m.?

Walker: Right, yeah. And then the rest of us. Especially of course when it was school time. And then on Sunday we got up in time to have breakfast and go to church. We usually had a hot breakfast of bacon and eggs or sausage and eggs or something like that, and hot biscuits. And then we'd get up and get ready to go to Sunday school. Sometimes he'd drive (the buckboard), but if it was summertime we'd probably walk because I remember a lot of times walking. You had one good pair of shoes. We'd walk barefoot up to church, and then we'd take socks and towels to clean our feet, and then we would sit down on the church lawn and put our shoes on and then we'd go into the church.

Hughes: That's just like what Adele Ferguson told in her oral history— the story about her little sister. They were heading for Bremerton from L.A. in the 1940s, all packed into one car. They were about an hour out of town when little sister said she had left her shoes at the park.

Walker: And they had to go back and get them. She found her shoes under a tree, and her little brother was sitting there. They'd forgotten and left him behind and didn't realize it. And he was sitting there crying. He said, "I knew you'd come back to get the shoes!" (laughing)

Hughes: I loved it! Mrs. Walker, you're so sharp. That's one of my favorite Adele stories. So, tell me about the chores that you would do. Would you gather the eggs?

Walker: Gather the eggs and cut kindling and sell wood. Dad would go down and get wood. We had to haul water a lot of times during the summertime because we lived a half mile from the creek and we had the big 50-gallon barrels.

Hughes: You didn't have any running water.

Walker: No. We had a couple of wells. But we hauled water to wash with. There was a barrel down on the barn lot for the horses. He had plenty of water there for them. But we had to haul water to wash and bathe and so forth. And we didn't water the lawn and the garden. No, you just let nature take care of that.

Hughes: You were saying you had a library table there in the evening. So, what were you doing there?

Walker: That's where we would study our school lessons at night.

Hughes: Were your folks a real stickler about the kids going to school?

Walker: Oh yes. Yes, *you had to go to school.* We had first through the eighth grade. You couldn't go to school until you were seven years old. I went to school when I was eight, however, because I was born in October—October 2nd.

Hughes: I'm on the 22nd.

Walker: Oh really? You're a Libra.

Hughes: I am a Libra. There's a little cutoff there. Are you a Libra too?

Walker: Yeah.

Hughes: I knew we were kindred souls.

Walker: I read the horoscope today.

Hughes: Is today a good day for us?

Walker: Today *is* a good day, and tonight—What did it say? "You're going to have fun tonight" or something like that.

Hughes: Well, there must be something to that. Maybe Nancy Reagan is right.

Walker: Well, you know maybe so. And another thing I believe in—and I think I get this from my grandmother, my mother's mother—is premonitions. Because I remember one time grandma said something about one of the boys—I think it was William Franklin. She told Mom, "That child is going to die before he ever gets grown." And he did. But you know, like, you can believe it or not. One day I was coming home and I put the key in the back door and a voice said to me, "You know, Lewis is going to die before you do." He was only a year and a half younger than me. I turned around and looked to see who was talking. So I just dismissed it but when Lewis got sick I said, "Well, Lord, you told me." My mother's mother, she was real telepathic. Grandma Mary.

Hughes: What kind of "telepathic" things would happen to her?

Walker: Well, that one thing about she told mom that that child was going to die. And he wasn't sick or anything. And the day before I broke my hip I had taken suitcases off of the shelf. I was looking for something and I couldn't find it. So I just said "forget it." About 3 that afternoon, here is this voice again, "You better put those suitcases up on the shelf or you'll fall and break your leg." I didn't do it.

Hughes: You should listen to those voices, Mrs. Walker!

Walker: When I hit the floor the next morning I heard my bone break, I just said, "Lord, I didn't listen." Because I'd been warned and I didn't do it.

Hughes: Was being a good Christian a big part of your family life?

Walker: *Oh yes*.

Hughes: So your folks were "foursquare" Christians?

Walker: Yes. Mom had been raised a Methodist but then she joined the church out in the country with dad. And when we went to town on weekends, on Sunday we went to Grandma's church—the Methodist Church. And I can remember this one thing after all these years: Grandma was a shouter. She would get up, walking across the front of the church and maybe make two or three trips across there. I remember Dad saying one time, "Well, I wonder if she'll be able to walk tomorrow?"

Hughes: I think it's really interesting how exuberant black church services are, but white folks are so uptight about that.

Walker: Well, we have a couple of ladies at our church that, oh Lord, you can hardly hear the preacher. "Amen!" "Praise it!" "Tell it!" "That's true!" "Right!"

Hughes: And you're not that way?

Walker: Heaven's no.

Hughes: You're more reserved. You're going to have private conversations with the Lord?

Walker: Right. You're right!

Hughes: We have another guest. (Alyce Eagans arrives) I am so pleased to meet you, Mrs. Eagans.

Judge Hunt: In the instructions I gave you on the way to come to Mrs.

Walker's house, it mentioned Loxie Eagans Boulevard. That was her late husband, who was a really fine gentleman.

Hughes: I was going to ask about your husband, because I figured that if there's a road named after him he must have done something really significant. What did Loxie do?

Eagans: He was the deputy EEO (equal employment opportunities officer) in the Shipyard and a community activist.

Walker: Yes, he was real active in the community and the NAACP.

> **EDITOR'S NOTE:** Loxie Eagans, who started work as a rigger helper at the Navy Yard in 1946, became the shipyard's first full-time deputy EEO officer in 1969. He had been chairman of the shipyard's Equal Employment Opportunity Committee, which was established in 1963. He was deputy EEO officer until his death in 1981. In 1988, the Kitsap County commissioners changed the name of K street to Loxie Eagans Way.

Hughes: Mrs. Walker, we were talking about your folks being strongly Christian, that it was a really important part of your growing up. Everybody went to Sunday school? Memorized the Bible?

Walker: Oh yeah, right. And even if you went to church during the week you had a Bible lesson. And so we were in church at least once or twice a week.

Hughes: What's the earliest thing you can remember as a child?

Walker: A lot of the real young age I don't remember. I have a nephew who says, "I can remember when I was born." I said, "You're lying because you can't remember that!" But I remember when I was first going to school. I couldn't go until I was eight, so I was always behind. Then when we moved to Stonefort and I went to this little one-room school there were four other girls in my class. I was in the third grade, and they never knew their lessons. They couldn't do math. They were bad at spelling. I led the class. So the teacher made a mistake. She put me in the fourth grade. She said, "I'm not going to let these girls hold you back." So, now, what I think she should have done was give me both third and fourth. But she didn't. So then when I got to the fifth grade, I flunked the fifth grade because I didn't get that math in the third grade.

Hughes: They pushed you too quickly.

Walker: Right. Then we moved back to Carrier Mills and I went on to the eighth grade there. We went to high school in Carrier Mills, and that was a mixed school.

Hughes: Mixed race you mean?

Walker: Mixed race, yes.

Hughes: So the rural school you had gone to that was mostly—

Walker: White. My brothers and I were the only colored children— and that was one of the first fights. When you got off the school grounds the teacher had no control over you. Well, this girl that lived right across the street from the school, her name was Hinshaw—Helen Hinshaw. She called me a nigger.

Hughes: How old were you then, Mrs. Walker?

Walker: I was in the third grade probably. This was when we went to Stonefort and there was a little one-room school and it went up to I think sixth grade. My brothers and I were the only non-whites. Once you get out on the street you're on your own. Helen called me nigger and I handed my books to one of my friends. Her name was Dimple Edwards. She was a white girl. Then I proceeded to "educate"—to take care of Helen. When we came back to school the next day things were different. She became one of my best friends. After that if somebody did wrong or mistreated my brother on the school grounds—that was Shirley—he didn't fight them because he was whiter than I am. So anyway, if anybody did anything to him she went and told the teacher. We didn't have to tell the teacher anything after that.

Hughes: So you had a real little "educational" session there, didn't you?

Walker: I had an educational session while I used my fists. I gave her a lesson—"You don't use that word!" When we moved here to Bremerton, Mom and Dad eventually came out here, too. Lewis and I got them out here. If some kid did something, my Mom would call them a "nigger." I said, "Mom, we don't use that word in this house." Because my kids were small. And I said, "We call people by their names or 'hey you' or whatever. But you don't use that word."

Hughes: Your mom, Hazel, was using that word just sort of as a label for somebody who was behaving badly?

Walker: That's right. You correct them but you don't use that word, no.

Hughes: I see a photo of a nice-looking man over there. And I see a lovely picture of you and James, your late husband.

Walker: The next one is my youngest brother, Ulysses, and his wife. And if you met them on the street you wouldn't know that they were colored people.

Hughes: Were there some shades of gray, so to speak, in terms of the way you were treated? Whether you looked dark or light-skinned?

Walker: It depended on where you were. When we first moved here in 1943, the mailbox was right out there on the road.

Hughes: Is this where you've lived for all these years?

Walker: Since May the 3rd, 1943. We added on to the house when we started having kids because we only had the bedroom, bathroom, and a small bedroom, and the living room, and this was the kitchen. And then we added on 20 x 34 feet.

Hughes: Did your husband do that work himself?

Walker: Oh no, we had a contractor. But when we first moved here and I went out to get the mail one day, there was two little boys playing in the dirt and they lived down at the end of that block there. And one of them said, "Are you nigger?" I said, "No, but your mother is." And so I never heard that word again. And we became friends. She never said one word to me about why did I say that. And that's all I said. I turned and got my mail and came on back to the house.

Hughes: You've been "educating" people for a long time haven't you, Mrs. Walker?

Walker: Well, I'm trying. I have tried. People have asked me, "Why do you do that?" I said, "If I'm going to live in a town, it's going to be like I like it or I'm going to move." In other words, they're gonna give or something's going to happen, one way or the other. When we first moved here, it snowed that winter, and we were on our way to downtown or something and we were on Burwell Street. There's quite an incline there. A police car was in front of us. So James got behind him to hold his car so he could get going in the snow. He reported to the chief of police that James had hit him. So the chief of police came to see us. He had come to arrest James.

Hughes: He was going to arrest James?

Walker: Yeah. The truth was that the man couldn't get his car going and he was slipping back. James came up behind him to give him traction so he could get going....People are funny. We worked in a theater, the Tower Theater downtown, doing cleaning. And most of the time we'd go in the morning before James went to work. And if the kids were asleep, we'd let them sleep in the car until they woke up and I'd go out and check on them. One evening we were eating dinner and the police came to the door. And he said, "Mrs. Walker?" And I said, "Yes." He had heard that we were neglecting our kids by leaving them in the car when they were sleeping. Well, I said, "You can come in and see for yourself if they're neglected." He looked at everyone at the dinner table and said, "They don't look neglected." And I explained that I checked on them every 10 minutes or so. If they were sound asleep, I'd let them sleep, but otherwise I'd bring them into the theater. We didn't neglect our kids. When they got older and if they had their homework done, they would help us on our janitorial jobs.

Hughes: At the peak of World War II there were some 32,000 workers at the Shipyard in Bremerton. Adele Ferguson authenticated that number for *The Bremerton Sun*. How many of those people were black folks or Filipinos, or otherwise people of color? A Navy document says there were 1,200 Negroes working at the Navy Yard in March of 1944, with another

900 by June. By the summer of '44 there were about 4,600, according to published accounts. The Kitsap County Black History pamphlet published in 1985 by Dianne's group says that at the peak of wartime activity there were 10,000 blacks here, which seems too high, based on Census records and other sources. Of course, a problem is that the war fell between 1940 and 1950. They only conduct an official Census every decade. The yearly estimates don't include race.

Robinson: I think that 10,000 number is pretty accurate. For one thing, it's just in most recent years that black people have been involved in the Census where you got a true accurate account of African-American people in any state. At one time, black people wouldn't even talk to Census people or they would give them really negative (or misleading) information. They were afraid to really say how many people there were in a household. So I really question the historical accuracy of Census records (from that era). Not only that, but we have to include blacks in the military, besides the black Navy Yard workers and the black workers at the torpedo station and Ammunition Depot—and the workers' families. I believe there were that many blacks here at the peak of the war effort. I've seen several references to there being that many (10,000).

Hughes: Then after the war, a lot of those black folks skedaddled to other places, didn't they?

Robinson: Yes. A lot of them went to Seattle. I talked to a lot them and they said, "Soon as the war was over, we left."...Maybe that number is a little on the high side, but I talked to the Housing Authority people, too. Black people were coming here in droves.

Hughes: Sinclair Heights, of course, was the segregated government housing project here in Bremerton, and then there was a black housing project in Port Orchard, too, wasn't there?

Robinson: Orchard Heights. I know there were 280 some housing units. But let me tell you what was happening within those units: If a person moved in and they had a person they knew in Texas who was wanting a job opportunity, they came up here and lived with those people. I know of three families that lived in one side of one of those duplex units. And that's how they did it—family and friends followed the workers who arrived, all of them coming for an opportunity...to make some money. They were really packed into a lot of those units.

Hughes: So it would be easy to extrapolate up to at least 8,000, wouldn't it? If we took the Navy's own figures just for the shipyard, not counting black people in the military here, and added in, say, another three people in a household—and in many cases a whole lot more ...

Robinson: That's right. A lot of people in one of those units. And they also had the "Duration Dormitories" for single workers.

Hughes: Well, all things considered, Dianne, I think you could easily make a case that if 10,000 was a little high, that 8,000 or 9,000 could have been easily reached. We found something on the Internet the other day that's pretty amazing. It's a report from Navy Intelligence about the civil rights movement in Bremerton in 1944.

Robinson: I have a quite a few of them, including that one. Declassified documents. They were even keeping track of which black people had guns. You should see all the documents I have—about blacks and whites fighting in the shipyard, white Marines attacking black people in a Chinese restaurant in 1945, without provocation, and the guards at the shipyard gate failed to take action. The Chinese man ordered the black people out of the restaurant. There were all sorts of incidents during that period of time. The black newspaper in Seattle called it "Nazism in Bremerton."

Hughes: This document here is amazing to me in its language. It's labeled "Confidential," and it's dated March 6, 1944. It was to the commandant of the Navy Yard on the "Negro Situation." They investigated the Puget Sound Civic Society: "Mrs. Lillian Walker, recording secretary," and, "John Dillon, sergeant-at-arms..." This is one of the most remarkable documents because in essence what it's saying is that the commandant wants to make sure the black folks aren't getting uppity. I mean, "What are they up to?" You should be incredibly proud of this, Mrs. Walker, because you're right in the middle of changing things here.

Walker: I would like a copy of that.

Hughes: I will get you one. The rallying cry for the Puget Sound Civic Society was to try to get rid of the "We cater to white trade only" signs around town. C.M. Stokes, a black attorney from Seattle, came and gave a talk.

Walker: He worked very closely with the NAACP. Mr. Stokes was a fine gentleman.

Hughes: Well, the Intelligence Office report has this to say: "On February 18, 1944, Mrs. Ozona Bonner, a Negro woman employed in the Navy Yard as a sweeper, slapped Mrs. Ruth Green, a white employee, in the women's locker room. For this act, the negress was suspended for three days." It doesn't say if anything happened to the white lady.

Walker: You know, the month that I worked in the Navy Yard there were three of us women, colored women. And I would get my work done and I would sit down. They'd say, "You better get to work." They would go in the restroom and hold their feet up off the floor so people didn't know where they were. And I said, "Well, if the boss comes, my work is done. And if he wants me to be working then he better give me some more work." Because you only had a few desks and stuff like that. And so I said, "No, I'm not going to go and run and hide. I don't have nothing to hide."

Hughes: How long have you known these ladies, Mrs. Walker (motioning toward Mrs. Eagans and Councilwoman Robinson)?

Walker: Oh Lord, I remember when Alyce was a girl. I knew her mom and dad, Lillian and Walker Wilson.

Eagans: I came in 1946. I was 16 because Mrs. Webb taught me piano.

Walker: You know, when somebody asks, "How are you today?" I say, "Today I feel like I'm about 150."

Hughes: Or my mother would say, "Ten years older than Methuselah."

Walker: We had a man in our church and I asked him one time how old he was. He said, "I'm two years older than God."

Hughes: That's funny! When did you come here, Dianne?

Robinson: I came in 1966. Originally I came from Maryland. I'm an

The Bremerton Naval Shipyard during World War II.

ex-Navy wife. And was traveling the East Coast and we got stationed out here in the Northwest. I'm originally from Florida.

Walker: My son was just in Maryland for a meeting....He's a Ph.D. Dr. James T. Walker.

Hughes: So your parents' emphasis on education really rubbed off on what you and James emphasized with your own children, didn't it?

Walker: Oh we went to school. If you had to walk a mile or three miles, you went to school.

Hughes: Some of us who are a lot younger like to tell our kids those stories about how we walked three miles to school, but you really did it.

Walker: We really did. The only time we got a ride to high school was if it was snowing so we couldn't walk. If it wasn't too bad, and school was open, Dad would get us in the wagon and take us to school. And when we went to town, Carrier Mills, he'd take us to town. And if it was real bad we would spend the weekend with Grandma Eddings. We had a great aunt that lived there, so we would split up and then we only had to walk like a quarter mile downtown to high school.

Hughes: When you were walking to school when you were a young girl you said you had one pair of shoes that you usually wore for Sunday.

Walker: I had a few more by high school. I kept my change and would add it up until I got enough to buy a pair of shoes. Or I'd give it to mom and dad.

Hughes: So, did you get an allowance or get paid for doing chores?

Walker: Are you kidding? *Nooooo!*

Hughes: How far away was the high school?

Walker: About three, three and a half miles. If the snow was too deep for him to get the horses out, well then we'd miss a day of school.

Hughes: How many kids went to the high school?

Walker: Oh Lord, you know I really don't know.

Hughes: A hundred children there?

Walker: Oh yeah. Because you had all the white kids. It wasn't a black school. It was a mixed school. But it was predominately white. But there were mostly colored people where we lived—and mixed race people, like I was telling you earlier. There was Uncle Joe Taborn. Now his wife, she looked like my grandmother. Some people said she was white. I don't know if she was mixed. But they had kids eventually. And Uncle Joe, he was not as white as she was. He was a farmer. We called him "uncle" because people

A black man poses with fellow shipyard workers during World War II.
Puget Sound Navy Museum.

A photo featured in the Shipyard newspaper, The Salute, shows a long line of job seekers outside the Labor Board Office on July 10, 1943. *Puget Sound Naval Shipyard*

who are as old as your folks you always call them either "aunt" or "uncle."

Hughes: That's what I was brought up to say, too. It was "Aunt Madge" and "Uncle Bill."

Walker: Right. Well that's the way it was back there.

Hughes: In terms of relationships between the high school kids—once you let people know what Lillian Allen was like, they might mess with you once but you did a lot of "educating" if you saw any overt acts of racism.

Walker: They didn't jump on me or my brothers, and if they did, they got a fist fight and I won.

Hughes: I don't think I gave you a chance to really fully answer my question about your father's personality. Tell us more about your dad. Was he a good-humored, friendly kind of guy?

Walker: Yeah he was. Sometimes you couldn't tell whether Dad was serious or not. But they were both strict. My mother and dad got up, like I told you, to make a fire in the morning. And we had a big pot-bellied stove, and he had to clean it out to get it ready for the day. One day there was no kindling. He went in my room, "Get out of that bed and go and get the kindling so I can make a fire!" If Dad told you to do something, you did it.

Hughes: And how about Mom? Was she a little more easy going?

Walker: You did what she told you to do because if you didn't, you know, "I'm going to tell your dad and he's going to come in and give you a whooping."

Hughes: Well, not only are you growing up in a rural part of Illinois where life is tough and there's no hot or cold running water, and there's an outhouse out back, all the classic stuff—but by the time you got to be 16 you're smack dab in the middle of the Great Depression.

Walker: Yeah. But we didn't realize it.

Hughes: Times were already so tough that you weren't that hard hit? You were growing your own food, raising chickens?

Walker: Oh yeah. The only thing you bought was flour, meal, and stuff like that because you had your vegetables; you had your potatoes, sweet and white. And sugar, salt, pepper—stuff like that.

Hughes: So the Allens didn't lose their car and their money in the stock market?

Walker: We didn't have any car and we didn't have any stocks, no sir!

Hughes: But were you aware generally that there were hard times all over America?

Walker: The only time that I *really* grasped it was when dad came

Bremerton at the height of World War II. Note the barrage balloon.
Kitsap County Historical Society Museum

home after he took this crate of vegetables to town, to Harrisburg, and he came home and he hadn't sold any. And mom said, "Well, what happened?" He said, "People don't have any money." So then we had to can that stuff or eat it because we just didn't throw food away, you know.

Hughes: One photo shows your Mom with her arm over your Dad's shoulder. Were they affectionate like that? You could tell that they loved each other?

Walker: Well, you could tell they loved each other enough—but Dad would get mad and fight with Mom.

Hughes: She sure looks sturdy. Did she hold her own in that?

Walker: No. She took it. But Lewis, my brother that came out here when he was 14 or 15, he once told Dad, "If you hit my mother again I'll kill you." And I don't think he ever hit her again.

Hughes: Good for Lewis.

Walker: That's right. That's what I say! When James and I were getting married I said, "I need to tell you something." "Well, what, honey?" And I said, "If you ever hit me, you better knock me out. Make sure I'm out cold, and be gone when I come to." "Honey, why?" I said, "Because if you're not, I'm going to kill you." "Honey, I wouldn't hit you! I love you." I says, "I know. I thought my dad loved my mother. But I'm telling you, I *will* not take a beating off of anybody." And one time when I was about 20, my boyfriend and I, we went to dinner. Charles, my boyfriend, was six foot, 200 pounds. I said something he didn't like, and he slapped me. Well, I hit him back. He said, "You little squirt you!" I said, "If you hit me, I'm going to hit you."

Hughes: I love this woman!

Walker: But the funny part is, in this little town the chief of police was a Negro and he knew Charles carried a gun. Charles had to not be caught with that gun so he'd give it to me. So I had left the gun in my room. And so when—

Hughes: Is this Bremerton we're talking about?

Walker: No, this is Harrisburg, Illinois. And so when we got to the door

I said, "Good night." And he went, "I bet you're going to kill me with my own gun." He thought I was going to get his gun and shoot him. I said, "You aren't worth the lead it would take to kill you with. So, here's your gun." I went on back to my room and I said, "Don't come back."

Hughes: You're really something, Mrs. Walker. This coal mining that dad did, was that kind of an intermittent thing? Because he's listed in the census in 1920 and again in 1930 as a coal miner and a farmer.

Walker: Yeah, he probably was. He didn't work every day, all the time, but he did work occasionally because he still had those 20 acres, you know, and he had his animals to take care of. And he had patch gardens—you know, a patch of potatoes here, sweet potatoes, and then we had corn.

Hughes: He pretty well diversified his crops.

Walker: He did.

Hughes: Was there any kind of county extension agent who came around to help you with that or did your dad just know quite a bit about farming?

Walker: He just knew. He was born a farmer, and he just knew how to do it.

Hughes: You were telling us that your father was literate. He could read and write.

Walker: And he was good in math. They both insisted that we go to school. You didn't dare miss a day of school. We didn't play hooky. And in my family if they got a whipping at school they got a whipping at home.

Hughes: We've lost some of that haven't we? You were more afraid of what your folks were going to do to you when you were a little snot at school?

Walker: *Oh*, you aren't a kidding! And so, grandma would come out, "Why don't you have your day clothes on?" "Well, I got a whipping at school and I'm waiting on you to whip me again."

Hughes: That's priceless. Did you have your nose in a book as a girl?

Walker: *Oh yes.*

Hughes: What did you like to read?

Walker: Everything. Mom couldn't read but I would read to her. Any magazine I'd found, or a book. I would read it to mom while she cooked dinner. I've always loved to read. But she couldn't read, so I would read to her. The Bible or whatever she wanted. Mom, "I got this for us." We didn't get any magazines because we couldn't afford them. I would read the newspaper to her.

Hughes: (Retired) Washington Supreme Court Justice Charles Z. Smith, whom you met the other day, said that his mother, who was the granddaughter of a slave, was always insistent, although she didn't have much schooling, she didn't want her children to speak in slang, or drop their g's, or say "ain't" or "gonna." Was that the way it was in your house?

Walker: If you said something not right, Dad would correct you.

Hughes: There was no profanity, no swearing?

Walker: Oh, Lord have mercy!

Hughes: What would happen if you swore?

Walker: You just didn't. I don't remember ever swearing when I was a kid. No. And you didn't use dirty language.

Hughes: Who do you think had the most influence on you as a girl growing up to be the kind of woman you are today? Who were *the* key people in your life?

Walker: Well, I had a great aunt, Amanda Williams. Sometimes I would stay the weekend with her. She was about the same age as my grand-mother—my mother's mother. And she lived about a half a block up the street. She had two granddaughters and they were about my age.

Hughes: If people called you a racial epithet you had all this gumption and gave them a licking. Who made you the kind of person you are? You're just so spunky, and you love learning, and you have this Golden Rule sensibility. Was there any one person there who was an important role model for you?

Walker: I was always encouraged to go to school. That and we didn't miss a day of school, unless you were sick. Now, if you had mumps or something—I could go hunting if I had mumps, but I couldn't go to school.

Hughes: You say go hunting, what did you go hunting for?

Walker: Rabbits, squirrels. Me and my dad would go hunting. I had my own .22 gun. I remember the first rabbit that I shot. I saw him sitting in the bushes. And dad said, "There he is." I got in front of him and shot a hole straight through him. I tore him up. He wasn't fit to eat. (laughing) But I learned, OK, you get around the side and shoot his head off.

Hughes: You don't want to ruin dinner. So you ate squirrels and rabbits?

Walker: Oh yeah.

Hughes: Was that stew stuff?

Walker: If it was a young one you fried it. And occasionally the dogs would tree a coon. We'd kill him, and my Mom, she'd roast him. Dad had hunting dogs. And if they smelled either a possum or a coon they'd go to the tree. Of course a rabbit, he was running.

Hughes: You were a pretty good shot then?

Walker: Yeah, I was. Dad had a .45 automatic, and New Year's Day, I was the first kid that got to shoot that gun. Nobody could wake you up. You had to wake up on your own. And the first one up got to shoot it.

Hughes: What happened on special occasions at your house? For birthdays or Christmas, what was a big celebration? What did you get on your birthday, for instance?

Walker: Mom would bake a cake. One Christmas—this will, I'm sure, give you an impression of our lives—us kids got an orange, or a banana, or an apple, or something like that. You didn't get any presents. One time, when I was probably 10 or 12 years old, dad needed a pair of underwear. So mom sent me to town; gave me a hen. I carried the hen to Carrier Mills, and sold the hen. Then I walked to the department store, and bought dad a pair of underwear. I bought him the most expensive thing they had. Mother asked, "Where's your change? Why would you pay so much?" I said, "Well, I got the best they had. So, I thought that's what you wanted."

Hughes: So you got scolded for buying the 25-cent underwear.

Walker: "Next time don't buy the expensive underwear!" "Well, you didn't tell me. You just told me to buy a pair of underwear, and I did."

Hughes: So, Christmas presents when you were a girl, you might get a piece of fruit?

Walker: Yeah, something like that. Or Mom knitted a pair of socks or something like that. We were poor. And like some people say, "We were very dirt poor."

Hughes: But, there was obviously something in that household where people had self-respect, and valued hard work and education.

Walker: Oh yeah.

Hughes: Would you say that the church had a lot to do with that?

Walker: Oh, I think so, yes. I believe church had a lot of influence.

Hughes: Some of the worst race riots and hateful things in America were happening when you were a child. 1919 has been called the "Red Summer" in America, in the South and the Northeast because there were so many lynchings and people being burned to death just because of the color of their skin.

Walker: Right.

Hughes: It was just incredible. So, in your relatively peaceful neck of the woods where racism wasn't an epidemic, were you aware of any incidents like that?

Walker: At one time there was because we lived right off one of the main highways going out to the country—Lakeview. And they dressed us in dark clothes. What had happened is that people made their own whiskey in those days, and a sheriff had gotten killed about five or 10 miles from where we lived, in the woods. They had found a still where people were making whiskey and the deputy sheriff went out there—silly fool, he went out there by himself and he got killed. And so they thought they had the man that killed him. And so they were coming through the county there in cars, the sheriff and police....We lived on the road and in back of us was a wood lot. I mean trees and stuff, and they took us back there. They put us in dark clothes.

Hughes: To hide you? You were in dark clothing to be hidden?

Walker: Yeah. Because they didn't know what these white people were going to do because they were up and down the road.

Hughes: Looking for the usual suspects?

Walker: They were looking for this man. But anyway, mom took us out there and dad stayed back at the house. So when they quit running up and down the roads in cars, and everything was quiet again, then dad came and got us and took us back to the house and we went to bed. That's the closest I've ever come to a race riot. Now, in Bremerton some white people thought there was going to be a race riot. It was in about 1954, I think, when James had sued this drug store man, down on 4th and Park, for not serving Negroes. Some white ladies from the NAACP—Peggy Gustafson, and I can't remember the other lady's name—they came to the meeting and they told us how to change things. This man had a soda fountain in there as well as a newsstand, and he served sodas and ice cream and stuff. There was a grade school up on the corner, about a block away. And the little colored kids if they went down and got an ice cream cone they had to go outside on the street, no matter what the weather was, but the little white kids could sit at the counter. This is wrong! The teachers found out about this and so they brought it to the NAACP and said we ought to do something about it.

Hughes: This happened in Bremerton in 1954?

Walker: At 4th and Park in Bremerton, Washington, in 1954. So that came up at the NAACP meeting. They decided to see if the druggist would serve a black customer. The attorney said to get plenty of witnesses. We had another friend about James' age, colored and everything, so they decided that James was going to sue him. So he and Whitt Johnson went down there and went right to the counter.

Hughes: His friend's first name was Whitt?

Walker: Whitt—Whittier. As a matter of fact they lived here with us for a few months because they couldn't find an apartment.

Hughes: Were they newcomers to Bremerton like you?

Walker: Yes, they were. There were from Ohio, I think. His wife still lives in Seattle and we talk every once in a while. In any case, James and

Whitt went down there, went in, and sat at the drug store counter. And the counter girl came up and said, "What will you have?" And they both said, "We'll have a milkshake or a cup of coffee," I can't remember which. She refused to serve them. Then the owner said, "I didn't serve niggers in Texas, and I'll go to hell before I serve them here." Well, he didn't know he was set up because we had white and black witnesses. We had already hired an attorney, Mr. Philip Burton, who was another prominent civil rights attorney in Seattle. And so James had all the witnesses and everything that he needed. And he sued him (in Kitsap County Superior Court). Well, he lost.

Hughes: Who lost?

Walker: The druggist.

Hughes: The *druggist*. OK. I was holding my breath there.

Walker: I'm sorry! But we got telephone calls at 2 and 3 o'clock in the morning, threatening us, saying what they were going to do. We better drop the suit, and all this negative stuff.

Hughes: What kind of things would they say? Were they just awful?

Walker: They were awful.

Hughes: For the historical record, do you remember anything specifically—the words that they used?

Walker: "We know you're in there! You niggers had better come out." Or something like that.…But we made a lot of white friends. We didn't care about the color of someone's skin. Our neighbors at that time were Ron and Ginnie Johnson, white folks. When they were moving in, James went over to see if he could help. Well, Ron said "No, I don't need your help." But it didn't take long before we became friends. James told Ron about these calls and about these cars driving by and Ron said, "Well, we'll have to stop that." So, they hooked up a connection that if they attempted to come in the house all James had to do was pull a cord or something. They had a signal going on. And Ron said, "We'll break this up."

Hughes: A cord. You mean they strung something across the street?

Walker: Oh yeah.

Hughes: Like we used to do when we were kids with the tin cans on twine?

Walker: Yeah. They had a big cord going across—an electrical cord.

Hughes: Oh, it was electrified. That's right because James, that was his job. He was an electrician.

Walker: That was his job, yeah. But it didn't happen (no violence). Thank God....Ron was set with his guns, too, so if they came here to attack us, he was going to (protect us). There was no need in calling the police because he was the police out here. And so finally it settled down. And we won the case. The druggist died a couple of years later. Now, I don't know whether he went to hell or not, but he died.

EDITOR'S NOTE: the case was settled out of court, with the store owners agreeing to cease discrimination. Philip L. Burton, 1915-1995, the Walkers' attorney, was instrumental in the desegregation of Seattle schools. He is in the National Bar Association Hall of Fame.

Phillip L. Burton
Washburn University School of Law

Hughes: I'm just struck by the fact of how far we've come in America.

Walker: Oh yeah. And years later, after we'd become really close friends, Ron said to James, "You know why I was so nasty to you when we first arrived?" Well, he was in the Navy and he'd been in the Philippines, and he'd just been through a race riot. So people carry these prejudices and opinions that can be broken down. I took care of their kids, and Ginnie took care of mine. Her kids called me "Mom Walker."

Hughes: Bill Cosby, the entertainer, has been really critical of black folks for letting young people and rap music artists use the "N" word. And he says, "I know that you're claiming that privilege, 'We can call ourselves that, but you can't call us that.' "

Walker: I don't like it for anybody in my race. And I would never let any of my kids say the word.

Hughes: So the notion of using that word in a popular culture kind of way, that doesn't ring right with you?

Walker: It does not.

Hughes: Because it still has that awful hateful, racist sting?

Walker: Why use it? You don't have to. You know when you say it that it's an insult to you. But we're talking about history here.

Hughes: Well, (asking Councilwoman Robinson) how does a young black woman feel about that?—Black people using the "N" word?

Robinson: I'll tell you what happened to me when I first came to Bremerton. The historical society had their annual banquet. I think they started in '42, so the banquet must have been when I was here in '60. And they had a song that they had made up. And the song said, "And they niggered all day." So my ex-husband—we were both were at this banquet, we had just come into the area—my husband got up, he's Navy, he gets up and says, "I have one thing to say. My wife is interested in history, and we love history. But you guys have to find a different word to use there instead of the word you used, 'And they niggered all day.' "

Hughes: Do you think they were trying to be funny, Dianne? Just ignorant?

Robinson: Just ignorant. I could tell you many, many stories that I have come upon. I remember one from World War II where they had this black lady, Mrs. Millie Williams, make bird outfits for all the little kids. And it was so beautiful because those kids looked so cute. But Mrs. Williams went to the program and didn't realize what was going on. The *black* kids had on these little suits that she had made, like little birds with the beak thing. And they were singing the song, "Black bird, black bird, through my window." And that's what the play was about. There was a big window on the stage decorated. And they had a little white girl with a little bonnet on her head…and they had the little black birds sitting across the stage and they had to go through the window, like "Black bird, black bird!"

Walker: I never heard that. Well, I'll be.

Robinson: Mrs. Williams said she was offended because she didn't know that she was making those (bird suits) for just the little black kids. You know, she thought she was making them for a play. So when she went to the program, all the black kids had them on.

Hughes: So they were stereotyping the little black kids?

Robinson: The little black kids, yes. But when I look at it I think, a lot of times people were just ignorant and didn't mean harm.

Walker: But it was degradating. And a lot of times they used ignorance as an excuse.

Robinson: And why would they not have put it on all of the kids—instead of on just the black kids?

Hughes: I know a young black woman who gets mad at black mothers giving their kids what she calls "made-up" names like Carmello and Shaquille. She said she keeps expecting to see a kid named Drixoral. There's even a study done about that, that made-up names can racially stereotype you and prevent you from getting ahead in the business world.

Walker: I never allowed my kids to have nicknames. They'd say, "How come we don't have nicknames?" I'd say, "If they have a name call them by their name." And someone said, "Well, you call Jimmy, Jimmy." I said, "I call him Jimmy because his daddy's name is James; his friend's name is James."

Hughes: Did your children ever insinuate to you that you were getting old fashioned about anything?

Walker: Oh, definitely, yeah. They'll say, "They don't do that any more mom." "OK, well, I do!"

Hughes: Tell me about high school. What was that like for you?

Walker: It was really interesting. A lot bigger school. We had classes in math, English, and physiology and at that point I was interested in nursing. So I didn't take typing, which I regretted later. But I was working on my history, ancient history. I just didn't study enough. And we had an old man who was a teacher. He must have been 70—almost thought of his name—he said, "Miss Allen, if you would study I'll give you the test over again." "OK." So I studied and took the test. I got a 90 on it. "How come you didn't do this during regular class?" I said, "I don't like history." Now I love math and reading, but I didn't like history. But I studied that. And so the rest of the time I made good grades because I realized I had to. You know, you can't skimp on this. You've got to study. So I did.

Hughes: Math was your favorite subject?

Walker: I loved math and I loved English.

Hughes: You can tell. You're very well spoken.

Walker: Thank you. And then when we came to Bremerton I took typing. James and I both took typing, and I took shorthand because I was supposed to use that, or so I thought. James and I took courses at Olympic College. Night school courses. That's when he got his first training in electricity. We took everything we could take that was going to help us in our work. I was going to go to nursing school. I had taken correspondence courses before I came to Bremerton. We had a doctor in Harrisburg that had a 13-bed home sanitarium, which included an operating room. So I went there after high school. And I asked him, "Dr. Lewis, I would like to apply for a job." "What do you want a job for? So you can make you some Easter clothes?" I said, "Well, I hadn't thought about that. I wanted a job." Well, he hired me. I started out as an office assistant. And I went from that to learning how to take your analysis, your blood pressure, take blood, give blood. And I learned how to run the operating room sanitizer. That's not the right word.

Hughes: Sterilization unit?

Walker: Sterilizer, yeah. And I learned how to do that. How to unpack it and everything. Then I learned how to assist in the operations. I have this letter from the doctor about my abilities.

EDITOR'S NOTE: The letter "To whom it may concern" from J.H. Lewis, M.D., attests that Lillian Allen worked at the Lewis Home Sanitorium in Harrisburg, Ill., from January of 1935 to September of 1937. She "very satisfactorily" performed duties in practical nursing, served as an office assistant, cook and dietician, as well as conducted urinalysis tests, checked patients' blood pressure and assisted in operations, "either giving ether or serving in the capacity of operative assistant." She was also responsible for post-operative care. "She has demonstrated a willingness to work hard and a fine type of intelligence, which coupled with her natural interest in medical work, should fit her for a successful career in nursing."

Hughes: Is this right after high school?

Walker: Yes. Right after high school. And worked my way up doing different jobs for him. He was a good teacher.

Hughes: What was the name of the high school you attended?

Walker: Carrier Mills High School. Some kids went on to college. I knew we couldn't afford college, my parents. And so, that's why I went to Dr. Lewis for a job.

Hughes: Was he a good man?

Walker: Oh he was—he was real good. So, I learned how to give ether as an anesthetic.

Hughes: And his first name was?

Walker: I think James. If I remember right. I only called him Dr. Lewis. He was a black man.

Hughes: You were getting real on-the-job training in practical nursing, weren't you?

Walker: I really got training. The only time that I messed up was one time when I was giving ether to a patient. I said, "Breathe in, breathe out, breathe in," and *I* went to sleep. The ether put *me* to sleep. I learned after that that you don't breathe when you're giving ether. I assisted him in operations. When he'd cut your gut open, I'd hold you open.

Hughes: Goodness.

Walker: And sop up the blood.

Hughes: So, you really had a stomach for that.

Walker: Right. Someone would say, "Doesn't the blood bother you?" And I'd say, "No. They could cut your head open, and then go and sew it back on. It's fine with me." It didn't bother me. As a matter of fact, one young man came in. He had been in an automobile accident. And his whole scalp, we had to peel his scalp back and clean his scalp before we could sew it back on. It didn't bother me *at all*.

Hughes: You should have been a doctor. You'd have been a great one.

Walker: Now, that's what I planned to do. Just before I came out here I had planned to go to medical school. I wanted to go beyond nursing because I knew I could do it.

Hughes: How long did you work with Dr. Lewis?

Walker: About three years

Hughes: And what happened after that?

Walker: I went to Chicago, to my aunt's, and I stayed there. With Aunt Carrie, Dad's sister. Carrie Inge. Then I met James Walker.

Hughes: Talk about cultural shock. You're going from Carrier Mills to Chicago.

Walker: Oh boy, you weren't kidding!

Hughes: Tell us what was it like? Were you just dazzled?

Walker: Yeah, I was. And it was really an education if you wanted to go downtown and see all the educational things… museums and the like. I worked for a private family, and the mother got sick in California. So they sent me to California to take care of her.

Hughes: So you were a nurse to a private family.

Walker: Yes.

Hughes: Was that a black family?

Walker: No, no. A white family,

Hughes: There were a lot of black folks in Chicago.

Walker: Yeah, well, this was in Oak Park, a suburb of Chicago.

Hughes: What did you think, by the way, when you saw Barack Obama in Lincoln Park on election night?

Walker: I just thought it was wonderful. Of course, the first time I heard Obama speak I said, "That's the man. *That is the man.*"

Hughes: So, they sent you to California with the family as a nurse-caregiver?

Walker: I went on the train to a place outside of Los Angeles. When I got there, she had died.

Hughes: Who was "she," Mrs. Walker? I'm sorry I'm not clear on this.

Walker: She was the mother of the family. The son and the daughter and their child were still there, and they sent me.

Hughes: So, when you got there the grandma had already succumbed?

Walker: Yes. So then they were sending me back to Chicago on the train, and they had a dilemma because here I'm black and she's white, and they're going to put me on the train. And they said, "Well, they'll just close the shades when they go through Texas."

Hughes: My God—literally?

Walker: Literally, yeah.

Hughes: So this is, what, 1936, '37?

Walker: 1938.

Hughes: 1938. So, you were working, in essence, as a private nurse?

Walker: Yeah, right. Well, I had the qualifications. I had started taking correspondence courses on nursing. And then I met James.

Hughes: From your correspondence classes did you get any formal equivalent, like an RN or LPN?

Walker: No, I didn't get that far. That was my next step and then I was going to go to medical school to be a doctor.

Hughes: What a great doctor you would have been with your compassion and common sense.

Walker: Well, I was told that as a kid. And one time we went to a

Sunday school vacation (program). We went to Metropolis, another small town in southern Illinois, and one of the teachers there came to me afterwards and he said, "You know, you ought to be an attorney. You've got a gift for gab." I said, "You're kidding. My folks can't send me to school to become an attorney." But anyway, I haven't done too bad.

Hughes: You haven't indeed. But you would have been a great doctor or attorney. Were there any kinds of programs for black kids to get into schools and colleges?

Walker: Not to my knowledge. I had one friend who went to college, and he tried to encourage me. I said, "I can't go to school. My parents don't have that kind of money. And both of your parents are working. You've got money."

Hughes: Well, you've done a lot to educate yourself.

Walker: Well, I've tried. You know, because when we first came to Bremerton we both took classes. Olympic College was the only higher school then. James started taking electrical classes. And then when he was working for AD.

Hughes: What's "AD"?

Walker: Naval Ammunition Depot.

Hughes: Was that just right down the road here?

Walker: It was right out here. But it's called Jackson Park now. It's a housing project now.

Hughes: We need to go back to Chicago where you meet this good-looking fellow—James Walker.

Walker: That's right.

Hughes: How did that happen? Tell me all about that.

Walker: A friend of mine was telling me about him. So I said, "Well, do you have a picture?" So, she gave me a picture of James. So we talked a lot and then I had to go to California. When I came back we talked more. Well, his mother and stepfather had moved to Seattle. And so he told me he was going to Seattle. And I said, "Well, OK." And he said, "Well, I want you to go with me." I said, "Well, I can't go with you. I'm working right now. But I can come later." So that's what happened. In 1940 I came. He was already in Seattle.

Hughes: You came out to Seattle in 1940?

Walker: Yeah, December of '40. And then we got married.

Hughes: When was that?

Walker: 1941. Most people remember their anniversaries. (laughing) We never celebrated an anniversary. We said we enjoyed each other all the time.

Hughes: This is the only chink in your armor: You don't remember the day you were married!

Walker: Isn't that something? But I remember the day we moved in this house—May 3, 1943. And people say, "How do you remember that and you don't remember your anniversary?" I said, "Well, we had an anniversary every day."

Hughes: That's wonderful. I like that.

Walker: We couldn't afford an anniversary.

EDITOR'S NOTE: Mrs. Walker looked up her wedding day after our interviews. It was May 20, 1941.

Robinson: Has Mrs. Walker been talking non-stop for two hours? (laughing)

Hughes: Yes she has. The first rule for every oral historian is "Shut up and listen."

Walker: You know, last Friday I was thinking about this interview and I said to myself, "This is too much. I can't handle this." I didn't know what I was getting into. (Agreeing to an oral history with The Legacy Project) I said to myself, "I'm over my head." Robin (Hunt) had given me these great papers of those people who'd had oral histories done earlier, including Judge Smith. And on there I found the oral history of Adele Ferguson (the longtime *Bremerton Sun* reporter and columnist). I read it. I don't think I went to bed until after 11 o'clock. I read the whole thing, except when she said she started at *The Sun*. I didn't read that because I already knew most of that.

Hughes: I have to tell you something really important, Mrs. Walker: I've been doing reporting and writing history for 43 years. I've interviewed three presidents of the United States, all sorts of important people. You're one of the most interesting and important people I've ever interviewed. You're not in "over your head." We want to tell the stories of people like you who have made a difference in their communities.

Walker: Oh goodness!

Hughes: What you have done is help change America. Judge Hunt told me when Attorney General Rob McKenna heard you speak, he said that it was as close to meeting Rosa Parks as he'd ever come. And it's true. What was really exciting for me was that you got to meet one of my heroes, and that's Justice Charles Z. Smith. He's a great man.

Walker: Yeah, he is. He told me, "I've read a lot about you. I know you." And I said, *"I know you!"*

Hughes: I told Adele I was going to interview you. I said, "Do you know a lady named Mrs. Walker?" And she smiled and said, "She's a livewire!" She also said that the black people in Bremerton were "first-rate folks."

Walker: (Laughs) I've been blessed in life to have really good friends.

Hughes: How long have you known Alyce Eagans.

Walker: Ever since she's been here. I met her when she was a child because I knew her mom and dad. They were members of our church.

Hughes: I meant to ask you, when you were growing up, if you followed politics—if your parents talked about President Roosevelt, Eleanor Roosevelt or—

Walker: One time we were in the wagon going from Carrier Mills to Stonefort. That's where we had to go to vote. And we met (a man) who asked dad, "Have both of you voted?" And Dad said, "That's where I'm

Lillian and James Walker on their wedding day in 1941.

going now." And Dad asked him, "Have you voted?" He said, "Yes." "Who did you vote for, Democrat or Republican?" "Republican." And Dad said, "Why did you vote a Republican? The Republicans have never done anything for the poor people. Why in the world would you vote for them?" That stayed with me. And when I got 21 and registered to vote, I registered Democrat. I just remembered those words, because I didn't know anything about politics. But if it was OK for him, it was OK for me. I didn't vote when I was in Chicago because we lived in Oak Park and I don't remember them ever talking about the election. But when I came out here (in early 1941) that's the first thing James and I did. We went down to the City Hall to see where we needed to register to vote. And while we were there, I saw a paper (poster) about insurances. The real estate man had said we couldn't get insurance. Well, I found out that we could. So I called him. I said, "You said we couldn't get insurance on this house." "Well, you're not in the city." I said, "According to the city map, we are in the city." So he went down and he called me back and he said, "I made a mistake."...And when we bought this place through the real estate man, we were going through the National Bank of Washington. And the banker's last name was Walker.

Hughes: No relation?

Walker: No.

Hughes: So, your identification early on was as a Democrat because your Dad was strongly for President Roosevelt and the Democrats?

Walker: Right.

Hughes: Did you follow any of the incidents that were happening in American life, like Jesse Owens at the Berlin Olympics or Joe Louis and his boxing matches with the German, Max Schmeling? Black role models.

Walker: Well, I knew who they were. They didn't impress me because I wasn't interested in sports at that time. My main thing was feeding my brain.

Hughes: You were talking about getting registered and buying this house.

Walker: Well, we got registered and everything. And then the bank wanted a thousand dollars as a down payment when we were buying this house. And so the real estate man, he said, "Well, I'll loan you a thousand dollars." So James and I agreed we would pay him back. Mr. Walker, the banker, said, "Do you know what you're doing?" And the real estate man said, "Yes, I trust Mr. and Mrs. Walker. They said they'd pay me and I believe them." And so, that's how it went.

Hughes: Do you remember what you paid for this house?

Walker: Thirty-three hundred dollars in 1943. We borrowed a thousand dollars, and we paid him back.

Hughes: That was a kindly act, wasn't it?

Walker: It *was*. It was a very kindly act.

Hughes: Was that guy just going on his instincts that you were good folks?

Walker: Yeah. James had met him and he had showed him the house. And in the conversation he liked us.

Hughes: Was that a white man?

Walker: He was a white man. People were impressed by our attitude. You know, James was teaching me how to drive and we went out to Keyport and I hit a man's car. I left a note on the car—my name, address, and phone number. On Monday he came to our apartment. And so he said, "I'm Al Segerquist. You hit my car and you left a note." I said, "Yes, I did." I said, "I'm sorry. And whatever the charges are we'll pay it." He was so impressed that I left a note, and left my address, and my name and everything. He said, "There are no charges, Mrs. Walker." And we became friends.

Hughes: You make friends in some amazing ways. You beat up Helen for calling you the N-word and you become friends.

Walker: Well, she was wrong. She said the wrong thing!

Hughes: I know. But this is another wonderful story.

Walker: But, Al one time he said, "Why are you always smiling?" I said, "Well, why shouldn't I be?"

Hughes: Stay on the sunny side, right?

Walker: I said, "Frowning and cursing, that's not going to make you any friends."

Hughes: Have you been that way since you were a girl?

Walker: I think so. Except if you were messing with me or something. And don't hit me.

Hughes: So, I was asking you about this good looking young man that you met—James Walker. What was James doing?

Walker: He had seen the ad in the paper about the Navy Yard.

Hughes: This was in Chicago when you met James Walker?

Walker: He was working out in Maywood. That's another suburb of Chicago. I think he was playing music because he had learned to play the saxophone from his mother, and he got in a small band and he was doing that.

Hughes: "Big Band" kind of stuff—a dance band?

Walker: Well, I don't know how big it was. Then when we got together and then he came out here. I told him, "I'm not going to marry a musician. I am not going to starve to death." "Well, I can get work." "But I'm not going to marry a musician." And he said, "Well, honey, I'm looking for another job."

Hughes: He could have been the next Count Basie!

Walker: Ooohhhhh. I didn't like that kind of stuff.

Hughes: You mean the nomadic life—the music scene?

Walker: I didn't like that. You know, when I first came to Washington State, a friend of his in Seattle came by the house and they had planned to go out that Saturday night, bar hopping. I said, "Well, you can do it, but when you get back I won't be here. I didn't come all the way out here to sit in the house and let you go bar hoping." So he went out to the car and he came back in. I said, "Oh, are you still here?" "Yeah," he said, "I told him I couldn't go."

Hughes: This guy is well trained. No wonder you fell in love with him. So, was this sort of love at first sight back then—Lillian and James?

Walker: It really was.

Hughes: What kind of a man was James? Did you call him Jim or Jimmy?

Walker: I called him James. He was nice, and he was not overbearing, and he tried to please. He was a gentleman. And people don't believe it, but we never had an argument in our life.

Hughes: Wait a minute, how many years were you married?

Walker: '41 to 2000, when he died.

Hughes: Never had an argument?

Walker: No. *Really.* People think I'm lying. No, we didn't argue about things. We discussed them, but neither of us got mad. If I was mad or something, I'd go downstairs or someplace, and then we'd continue the discussion.

Hughes: Sort of go to neutral corners and cool off?

Walker: Right, right.

Hughes: That's probably a good thing to do.

Walker: I always thought so. We discussed things. The only thing he ever went and bought that we didn't discuss was a camera. One day I was out in his workshop and I saw this camera hanging on the corner. I said, "What's this?" "Oh honey, I did something that I shouldn't have done." I said, "What do you mean?" "I bought that camera and I didn't ask you or tell you, and we didn't discuss it." I said, "Well, if you've got enough money to pay for it …"

Hughes: Was it a pretty nice camera?

Walker: It was. It was two hundred and some dollars. I said, "OK, I'll take it out of your allowance." He didn't have an allowance. But that's the only thing that either one of us ever bought and didn't tell the other one.

Hughes: So, what was James' background? Was he an Illinois boy?

Walker: Oh yeah, he was from the outskirts of Cairo, Illinois. But we didn't know each other. That's 60 miles from Carrier Mills, and we didn't know each other. I didn't meet him until a friend of mine from Carrier Mills met him in Maywood and she told me about him and then we met. And so we liked each other from the get-go. I said, "Well, that's fine. If you don't like me just say OK." And he said, "No, no, I like you!" I said, "OK, I like you." So we finally got married. And one time when we working at the shipyard they were going to send him to Louisiana, some place where they needed help—an electrician.

Hughes: Permanently or was it just temporary duty?

Walker: I think it was temporary duty. We had been to Monroe once, where James lived for a while, and I had gone to the store to buy a pair of hose. And the clerk—

Hughes: Monroe, Washington?

Walker: No, Monroe, *Louisiana*. And she stopped waiting on me when a white man came in. Well, I went to the car and waited out in the car. I said to James, "Would you get me out of this town because otherwise I'm going to kill somebody." So one day he told me they wanted to send him down South— I think it was Louisiana. And he said, "But I hate to take you down there." I said, "Don't worry about that. We'll either straighten out the town or we'll move!"

Hughes: You are just amazing.

Walker: But they never did send him.

Hughes: What gave you your wonderful sense of self-esteem, where you always just thought, "I am somebody"?

Walker: I've always liked myself. And I always said, "Well, you're either with me or against me. And if you're against me, that means we're going to have to fight."

Hughes: So, what was James Walker's personality?

Walker: He was quiet.

Hughes: Has anybody ever accused you of being quiet?

Walker: No! (laughing) Speaking of being quiet—I was on a trip with my church.

Hughes: Which church is that?

Ebenezer A.M.E. Church in Bremerton

Walker: Ebenezer A.M.E., African Methodist Episcopal— colored people. And so, the pastor, she said, "Mrs. Walker, I want to take you off the trustees and I want to put you as a trustee emeritus." I said, "And why do you want to do that?" "Well, that's an improvement." I said, "That's not an improvement to me. That's a demotion. You want me to shut my mouth." I got words, "If you think you're going to shut me up, you're wrong—because I'm a member of this church, and I'm putting my money in there, and I'm going to speak. Whether I'm right or wrong, whether I'm for you or against you, you will know how I feel." Well, it didn't happen, she didn't make me "emeritus."

Hughes: You're not ready to be kicked upstairs.

Walker: *No!* When God gets ready for me, well, he can come whenever he wants. But I think this lady, I don't know, she hasn't said anything else to me. She's different. Lord have mercy, she's different.

Hughes: You know, I'm looking at your husband's smile in that photo over there. James had a thousand-watt smile didn't he?

Walker: Yes, he did, he had a beautiful smile.

Hughes: Was he a short guy, someone said?

Walker: Yeah.

Hughes: How tall was James?

Walker: He and I were about the same height. I believe he was a couple of inches shorter—if I had on heels.

EDITOR'S NOTE: Mrs. Walker's son says his father was 5-6.

Hughes: So, there you are in Chicago. You're real serious about this fellow, and he says, "I'm heading out to Seattle." And you made certain that he was serious about this, too, and then you high-tailed it for Seattle as well.

Walker: Yeah. I came out on the bus. He wanted me to fly out. I said, "I flew to California. I went back to Chicago on the train. I am going to come out on the bus so I can see part of the country."

Hughes: Greyhound.

Walker: Yeah, and it was a good trip.

Hughes: I'll bet it was. So, what was James doing in Seattle?

Walker: He was working for somebody that helped clean passenger cars, or something like that. But then he got a call. His mother was working for a private family and she met this lady that lived in Longview. And they were looking for someone to work for them. So, James and I went down to Longview, Washington, and worked for them. And we told them that they had a job opening in the Navy Yard but he hadn't received his card yet. A funny thing happened down there in Longview. James was a yard boy and a chauffeur. And he was in the flower beds. There was a little white boy that lived next door. And he saw James pulling weeds and he said, "How come your hand's darker than mine?" See, he had not been brainwashed.

Hughes: He had not been inculcated with prejudice.

Walker: No, he hadn't, no. And James said, "That's my color. I'm that color all over."…The couple, Mr. and Mrs. Hatch, had milk delivered. So one day when the milk man came, it was strawberry season, and I said, "Can I buy a pint of whipping cream?" "Sure." So I bought it and put in it in the refrigerator. Well, she mixed it with milk. And I said, "Mrs. Hatch, did you see my whipping cream?" She said, "We don't have any whipping cream." And I said, "OK." So when the milk man came I said, "Will you come to the door, Mrs. Hatch?" And I asked him in front of her, "Did I buy a pint of whipping cream from you last week?" "Yes you did." "Ok, thank you."

Hughes: Did she get the message?

Walker: She got the message.

Hughes: What did she say? Was she apologetic?

Walker: Are you kidding? *No.*

Hughes: You have never been willing to settle for being a second-class citizen.

Walker: No. That's what she was trying to treat me like.

Hughes: What were your duties when you worked for that couple?

Walker: My duties were to take care of the house, do the cooking. One day I fixed dinner and James had changed clothes and cleaned up. And he'd take the food in and he'd serve them. He'd give them what they want. He'd come back out: "Do they want anymore?" "That's all I gave them."

Hughes: So, then did James end up getting his slot at the shipyard?

Walker: Oh yes. When he got the call then we told them we had to leave.

Hughes: When was it that your husband got the call to come to work at the shipyards?

Walker: It was in late May of '41. We came to Bremerton on June 20, 1941. Isn't that funny—I can remember that, but I can't remember my anniversary....We stayed in an apartment down on 8th Street. We lived in the basement where you had to walk up three floors for the bathroom. So then we heard of Dick Turpin, a fine gentleman....He had this apartment house on 4th and Park. You had the bedroom and you divide the kitchen and bathroom with two other couples. And so he said he had a couple that was moving out in a couple weeks. So we moved there and stayed there until '42.

EDITOR'S NOTE: Retired Chief Petty Officer John Henry "Dick" Turpin worked as a rigger/diver in the Navy Yard after his retirement from the Navy in the 1920s. "Tall, erect and courtly," he was one of the most highly respected blacks in the history of Kitsap County and is fondly remembered. His amazing stories had the added advantage of being true. A strong swimmer, he survived the explosion that decimated the battleship Maine in Havana Harbor in 1898, and is credited with saving the life of the ship's captain. Dianne Robinson of the Kitsap County Black Historical Society believes he is entitled to a Congressional Medal of Honor.

Chief Petty Officer
Dick Turpin.
Puget Sound Navy Museum

Hughes: Were there any kind of racial issues there in the living accommodations?

Walker: No, we didn't have any because the other two couples were Negroes.

Hughes: But were there white folks and black folks living in the same apartment house?

Walker: No, we were all black couples.

Hughes: So the Bremerton you moved to, in a lot of respects, was a more segregated society than what you were used to.

Walker: I wasn't used to it. I'd never been to any place where I'd been refused because of my color or my race....I think the first time we really saw it was when we went out to eat. There used to be a restaurant on 2nd Street, beyond where Penney's was, and we went in there for dinner.

Hughes: Do you remember the name of that place, Mrs. Walker?

Walker: No, it was a café on Burwell. I don't remember the name of it. And the waitress, after a half an hour of waiting, she came out and said, "Well, I'm sorry, I can't wait on you because my boss said it's because of the color of your skin." Or something like that. She didn't call us Negro, or nigger, or anything like that. So we asked her why, and she told us. So we left. And then after that, someplace else had a similar experience. All the restaurants up and down Pacific, the main drag, were the places that served hamburgers. A Navy man, a black individual in garb, you know— this sailor went in one place and ordered a hamburger. This restaurant had a black man, like a native, on its window. And he had a hamburger in his hand—you know, half dressed.

Hughes: You mean like an African native?

Walker: Yes, right. The black sailor went in and ordered a hamburger. They said, "We don't serve niggers in here." He said, "I don't eat them either. But I want a hamburger."

Hughes: You say there was a picture in the window of an African native?

Walker: Yes.

Hughes: Half naked, eating a hamburger?

Walker: Right.

Hughes: Sort of like the "Coon Chicken Inn," huh?

Walker: Yeah.

Robinson: You know about "Coon Chicken"?!

Hughes: I do. Their logo was a grinning, stereotypical caricature of a Stepin Fetchit Negro.

> **EDITOR'S NOTE:** Here are two links:
> http://en.wikipedia.org/wiki/Coon_Chicken_Inn
> http://www.ferris.edu/jimcrow/coon/

Robinson: I've got a box down there (at the museum) with "Coon Chicken." And there were Sambo's restaurants, too.

Hughes: Was there a "Coon Chicken" restaurant in Bremerton? I know there was one in Portland.

Robinson: Not in Bremerton, but they had one in Washington.

Hughes: But in this story we're talking about, they had a picture in the window that featured an African native—

Walker: With a hamburger in his hand.

Hughes: Sort of like a savage.

Walker: Yeah, right.

Hughes: That stereotype. That's incredible.

Walker: The sailor said, "I don't eat them either. But I want a hamburger."

Hughes: I don't eat what? You mean like cannibals?

Walker: Yeah, right.

Hughes: So he was referring to the sign?

Walker: Right. The hamburger place was down on Pacific between Burwell and First Street, just a little hole in the wall. I don't even know if you could sit down.

Hughes: Did that attitude pervade society in Bremerton or was it just sort of isolated?

Walker: Oh yes it was. Ben White, who used to be a policeman, was a white man but he was nice. And James heard this white sailor tell him, "You're a nigger lover!" And Mr. White said, "No, I just like people." We were working at the theater at that time.

Hughes: Which theater was that?

Walker: The Tower on 4th Street.

Hughes: Is it still there?

Walker: I don't think so. I think there's a school there or something.

Hughes: Okay, the Tower Theater on 4th. Were you ushers?

Walker: No, we were cleaners—we cleaned everything. They had this marble entrance, so James was mopping that one day and these two sailors came by and jumped him and started fighting him.

Hughes: Unprovoked?

Walker: Unprovoked. No words exchanged. So the policeman I just mentioned, he broke it up. And that's when the sailor called him a nigger lover. He took him to jail because he had seen the whole thing. So James didn't have to appear or anything.

Hughes: Strike one blow for justice.

Walker: Right. And the next thing was that we went to the NAACP meeting (and talked about the incidents). And a white friend of mine was there, and this man said, "And what are you doing here? This is the NAACP." And I said, "She's a friend of mine and I invited her."

Hughes: This is a white person. Why object to her being there?

Walker: Lord have mercy!

Hughes: Was it actually at that time called the NAACP or did it have an earlier name in Bremerton?

Walker: No, it's always been.

Hughes: I am confused, ladies. Was there a Carver Club?

Robinson: That was the women's club.

Hughes: Ok. I thought I had read something to the effect that that the Carver Club was quote, "a forerunner" to the NAACP. But there was a full-fledged chapter of the NAACP?

Walker: Yes. We went to Olympia and Seattle for assistance in founding a chapter here. We had help from Seattle, and we went to Olympia and got the charter. Mr. and Mrs. Colvin, and Mr. and Mrs. Greer, and James and I helped establish it. I can't remember all the names…

Hughes: So, you and James were charter members of the Bremerton Chapter of the NAACP?

Walker: Yes.

Robinson: It was chartered on May 23, 1943.

Walker: James was the second president of the NAACP here, after the Rev. (Chester W.) Cooper, pastor of Ebenezer A.M.E. I was the secretary and we built it up to 500 members. I used to hand-address and send out all those notices for our meetings, and we paid the postage, too, although it wasn't much back then for a postcard.

Robinson: And Mrs. Walker was also state secretary for the NAACP in the 1940s.

> **EDITOR'S NOTE:** Robinson informed us later that Puget Sound Civic Society, also referred to as the "Town Forum," was an outreach effort by the Bremerton branch of the NAACP. It included people of all races who worked to abolish discrimination and build a better community.

Hughes: Dianne, I think that in some of the historical work that you've done that I read that there had been black people working at the Navy Yard, several hundred of them, as early as 1909, 1910. Is that right?

Robinson: Yes, that's true.

Hughes: And were they drawn to work here when the Navy Yard began to be this going concern as America built up its fleet of warships?

Robinson: Yes.

Hughes: So when James and Lillian Walker arrived in Bremerton in June of 1941, how many black and other minority folks would there have been here? I understand there were a lot of Filipino people, too.

Robinson: There were quite a few. In all, probably 2,000 people of color in the county and 1,000 at the Ship Yard. But back when the Ship Yard first started, it said in a newspaper article that a "colored" restaurant had opened up in 1909. And they gave the names of the owners, and what have you. And they said that they had opened that restaurant to cater to the 200 colored workers who were in the Ship Yard at that time. During World War I, there were a lot of colored businesses in the downtown area—well, I shouldn't say "a lot," but I could come up with at least five or six of them that were actually in the downtown Bremerton area. And all of the black folks during that period of time were pretty much in that area—Park, 5th Street, 4th Street, all of that area.

Walker: Right.

Robinson: This was during World War I.

Walker: There was a project over there either on 5th or 4th, someplace in there, up from Park, they were mostly Negroes.

Robinson: Right.

Hughes: The peak employment during World War II was 32,343 "on a day in July of 1945," according to Adele Ferguson. She vividly remembers asking a Navy official for the number and committing it to memory. Other sources say it was "nearly 34,000," but I'll bet Adele's number is correct. She's a stickler for details.

EDITOR'S NOTE: "The Navy Yard set a goal of 36,000 workers but for many reasons was never quite able to reach it," according to "NIPSIC to NIMITZ, A Centennial History of Puget Sound Naval Shipyard," by Louise M. Reh and Helen Lou Ross (ISBN 0-931475-02-3). "Instead of coming to the Navy Yard, local workers with experience sought higher paying jobs in the burgeoning aircraft industry and well established shipbuilding plants in Seattle. A dearth of housing in the Bremerton area, or a long ferry ride...discouraged workers from applying at PSNY. Something had to be done…" Two naval officers "recruited throughout the state, using movies, radio and press to attract workers.…A national campaign to attract 7,500 journeymen and helpers was begun through the Civil Service Commission. A month spent in Minnesota by recruiters resulted in 3,838 workers reporting to the Navy Yard. During the first part of July 1943, as many as 300 persons a day arrived" at the Navy Yard. Housing was in short supply. By August of 1942, it was estimated that 2,500 families lived in trailers. "Garages and chicken coops were remodeled. Defense workers slept in cars, tents, basements and attics. Rooming houses featured 'hot beds' where three shifts of workers kept the sheets warm.…Families doubled up, commuted from Seattle or took housing wherever they could find it."

War-time workers lived in trailers, shacks, even chicken coops, as they poured into Bremerton in 1942. Note the barrage balloon on the horizon. The balloons were tethered to the ground by steel cables that could slice the wings off low-flying enemy aircraft.
Puget Sound Navy Museum

Walker: When we were living at the apartment, a man across the street—a colored man—he worked out at Kitsap Lake. This lady had a night club out there. They wanted an assistant cook, so he would take me to work every night. One night, there was a white man who was on this side of the bar—of the counter—and he threatened me. He was going to come across the counter and get me. I said, "Well, that's fine." I had this big long butcher knife. So I said, "You come right ahead. I guarantee you'll leave with less than you came over here with." I told the cook what the man said. And he said, "Well, let him come on. I'll help you." So, needless to say, he went on to the bar, got him a drink and went wherever he was going. I didn't have any more trouble because I wanted the word known, "If you attack her she's going to kill you!" (laughing)

Hughes: So, you and James hadn't been here but a couple of months when you saw that this was a place where racism was—

Walker: It was running rampant.

Hughes: I understand that among Negroes there was some resentment against newcomers from the Deep South whose manners were not as good.

Walker: Oh yeah. Right.

Hughes: They just weren't as cultivated?

Walker: No. To my observation, they had never been around white folks much.

Hughes: Their manners and whole ability to interact around white folks was different?

Walker: I think so, and I was criticized a lot of times for socializing with whites?

Hughes: By black people?

Walker: Oh yeah.

Hughes: Talk about "reverse discrimination"!

Walker: Right! (laughing)

Hughes: And I read somewhere that even the white locals were drawing a distinction between northern blacks and southern blacks.

Walker: I believe so because I had been told several times by white people "You don't sound like you came from the South," and I said, "I didn't come from the South. I came from Illinois."

Hughes: When you arrived, did you find kindred souls immediately among other people of color who were outraged?

Walker: We made friends—white and black. I met a lot of white people who weren't racist—women who I helped start the Church Women United. That was women from every church, black and white. At one time we had about 150 members.

Hughes: Really? That's wonderful.

Walker: But since I broke my hip, the then president called me and said, "Well, we're going to disband the Church Women United because we're only getting five or six people to come to the meetings." I said, "Well, I can't come, so whatever you guys do. I'm not the president or anything." So it disbanded.

Hughes: So, early on, when you formed the NAACP Chapter here, was that a reaction to the overt signs of discrimination? Those blatant signs, "We cater to white trade only"?

Walker: That was part of it. I knew that with the NAACP you would have all races fighting for civil rights. And that's why we formed it—to change things here. We talked to people in Seattle that were in charge. We knew that we needed help. It was just more than two or three of us that were fighting could do by ourselves.

Hughes: Who were some of the key people who were involved with you and James in the NAACP?

Walker: Mr. and Mrs. Al Colvin. He's dead, but Hazel is still living. And Mr. and Mrs. Greer, Elwood and Marie, and they're both gone. The Eagans were involved with the NAACP. Loxie's gone now, but we still have Alyce. I don't know if I can name all these people.

Hughes: Who were some of the righteous white folks who were really standing up with you? Do you remember any of their names?

Walker: I can remember their faces. I can't remember their names. One incident I remember is that we'd been to the NAACP meeting at the

YMCA. I was the recording secretary. There was a little restaurant coming out of the Navy Yard. It was called the Triangle Café. Anyway, we went in there to get a cup of coffee and a piece of pie. Whatever, you know. Peggy Gustafson and I were together. Peggy was a white woman who was active in the NAACP, together with another white lady whose name I'm sorry I can't recall. We went in, and there were several others that came in. The waitress asked Peggy what she wanted. And Peggy told her, "I'll have whatever Mrs. Walker is having." So I said, "I'd like a piece of pie and a cup of coffee." And the waitress went around the corner of the U-shaped counter and didn't serve us. So I got up and followed her around. I said, "I told you I wanted a piece of pie and a cup of coffee." She said, "Well, I've only got two hands!" I said, "Well, you're not using either one of them....What's your name and your phone number? And what's your boss's name?" Well, she darted right out the door. There was a telephone booth right in front of the restaurant. And my brother, Ulysses, who was 16 years old, was standing next to the phone booth waiting on the bus to come home because he worked at the YMCA. The waitress called Art Morken, who was the chief of police, and told him that there was about to be a race riot. So the chief came down to the restaurant and asked, "What's going on?" And we said, "We just stopped in here to get something to eat—a piece of pie and a cup of coffee." Well, the chief and Bill Simmons of the NAACP set up a meeting, and our minister was there, too. And they met on Monday because the incident occurred on Sunday. Well, the man who owned the restaurant decided that he'd take down the "We serve whites only" signs and that he'd serve anybody that walked in the door.

Hughes: He was persuaded.

Walker: *He was persuaded.*

Hughes: Do you remember the gentleman's name who got turned around on his attitude?

Walker: I don't remember.

Hughes: Did he really have a change of heart?

Walker: Well, he didn't fight it. He agreed that he would open the

Bremerton Police Chief Art Morken in the 1940s.

restaurant to anybody that walked through the door.

Hughes: So, of course you tested that.

Walker: That's true! (laughing)

Hughes: Was he cordial after that?

Walker: Yeah, we didn't have any problems after that.

Hughes: And how about the police chief?

Walker: Art Morken was a nice guy. He was a good white man! (laughing)

Hughes: I'm glad to hear that. I was feeling like I'd be the Lone Ranger here in 1942!

Walker: I know what you mean. But Art was chief for years and well respected.

Hughes: Dianne, does Mrs. Walker have it right? Was Art Morken a stand-up guy?

Robinson: Yes he was.

Hughes: And what was the reputation of the Bremerton Police Department generally? Because of Chief Morken were they pretty even-handed with people of color?

Walker: I think so. I don't believe that he would have put up with it.

Hughes: So, you had cafés and barber shops and drug stores with "Whites only" signs?

Walker: Oh yes! Let me tell you more about the barber shop.

Hughes: Absolutely. I want to hear all about the barber shop.

Walker: It was over on Callow Street. Let's see, let me get my directions right. It was south on Callow, and right, almost on the corner. So we stopped in there because James wanted a haircut.

Hughes: Do you remember the name of the place?

Walker: No. But James told the barber he wanted to get a haircut. And the white man said, "Well, if you come back after 5 o'clock, we'll close the shades and I'll cut your hair." I said, "You won't cut his hair after 5 o'clock if you're going to pull the shade. Because I am a barber and I *will* cut his hair, so you won't have that problem anymore."

Hughes: He didn't want anyone to see him cutting a black man's hair. Don't want to shock the neighbors!

Walker: If he couldn't cut a black man's hair in bright daylight, there was no way we were going to go there. So I said to James, "Excuse me, honey, you will not be back after 5 o'clock. We will not go anyplace that the shade is closed. No, if you're going to cut his hair, you'll cut it right now, because if you don't cut it, I will cut it when I get home because I *am* a barber." I had been trained as a barber back in Carrier Mills.

Hughes: Wow. You're a nurse, you're a barber, you're a cook, and you can hoe and plough! So did you cut James' hair from then on?

Walker: Yes I did. I cut James' hair. I cut my brothers' hair. I cut my son's hair.

Hughes: Ulysses. Did another brother come out here, too?

Walker: Yes. Lewis. Ulysses came here and graduated from high school here. He visited and then went back home and he told mom and dad, "I want to go back to Washington." And so he got him a job and went to work and paid his way out here.

Hughes: I'm confused about one thing.

Walker: What's that?

Hughes: Your brothers' names: There's Shirley, there's Lewis, there's William, there's Ulysses… (on the Census records)

Walker: Let me see that.

Hughes: This is the 1920 Census. Let me go to the 1930. Records. On this one we've got Moses, and Hazel, and Lillian, and Lewis, and Damon. And the boys who came out here to Bremerton were Ulysses and—

Walker: And Lewis. Shirley came briefly. He had nine kids at home, and he said, "I'll never get all those kids out here." He came to visit, but he went back to Carrier Mills.

Hughes: You have a complicated family, Mrs. Walker.

Walker: Now, when my son got a scholarship to Stanford, I told him, "I have one thing to say: Don't bring me any grandkids unless you've found the right girl and get married." And so he didn't, thank God.

Hughes: Your son got a scholarship to Stanford? That's about as good as it gets!

Walker: Well, we thought so.

Hughes: You should be very proud.

Walker: He told me about four or five years ago, "Mom, when I was in my teens I knew that I wanted to be a Ph.D." I said, "Well, you never told me. I knew you wanted to go to college." So, his freshman year at West High, he brought home his report card. He handed it to me, and it had an "F" on it. And I said, "I thought you wanted to go to college." "I do." And I said, "Well, you'll never get into college with an 'F' on your card. Now, tell me why it happened." "Well, I didn't turn in a book report." "Why?" "I didn't want to read the book." I said, "That's not an excuse. If you have another 'F' on your college ap you're not going to make it."

Hughes: Absolutely.

Walker: He graduated with a 3.8 average.

Hughes: So, when did children start arriving to James and Lillian Walker?

Walker: Jimmy was born in 1945, August 29th.

Hughes: Is that James Jr.?

Walker: Yes. It was the happiest day of my life.

Hughes: What's his middle name?

Walker: Titus. It's out of the Bible.

Hughes: That's a great name.

Walker: I have one great-grandson—my daughter's grandson—and his name is Titus James.

Hughes: So how many grandchildren are there now?

Walker: Jimmy has two girls and a boy and June also has three kids—a boy and two girls.

Hughes: So six in all?

Walker: Yes, and I have three great-grandchildren.

Hughes: So, James is your first child. Who comes next?

Walker: June. We adopted her when she was eight months old in 1950. I had lost three girls. I lost one within two weeks of full term. She was born dead. And then I lost twins at six months.

Hughes: Oh my goodness. I'm sorry to learn that.

Walker: The doctor was trying to get me to six months. He said, "If I can get you two or three days over six months then we can get them in the incubator." Well, my labor started about two days before six months. And I went to the hospital. One of them was already dead, and the other one died before we could get her to the incubator. And the doctor said, "If you ever decide to have another kid you get you another doctor because I'm not going to carry you through any more." So I said, "OK. What do we do about it?" "Well, we can tie your tubes." I said, "OK, let's do it." So, then we adopted June at eight months (in 1950).

Hughes: Lovely.

Walker: Sometimes I think *she* thinks it was a mistake. But she's been real good to me when I came out of the rest home.

Hughes: You mean in the wake of breaking your hip?

Walker: Yeah, right.

Hughes: You're so lucky. A lot of older people, breaking a hip, that's a death sentence.

Lillian and June in the 1950s.

Walker: That's what one of the clerks at the Safeway store said. If he's working I try to go to his counter because he knows me. And he said, "Mrs. Walker, you look fine, you're walking." I said, "I am doing fine, but I'm not doing as good as I'd like to be doing." He said, "Don't complain. My mother had her hip operated on at 80 and she hasn't walked since." When I took therapy, I complained one day about something. And one of the young men said, "What are you complaining about? Here you are 90-some years old and I have people in here that are 60 that can't do what you're doing." I said, "OK. Excuse me. I won't complain anymore!"

Hughes: Do I understand that your parents moved out here, too?

Walker: Yeah, in '65, Mom and Dad moved out here. They only had one son back there, and so they came out here. When dad died in '66, we had a room downstairs, and we had a washroom with a sink, and a toilet, and a shower. And I said, "Mom, we will finish this and turn it into an apartment." She said, "I don't want to live with you and James. I don't want to live with Ulysses. I don't want to live with Lewis. So we got her a room at West Park, an apartment, and she just loved it. Because there were four in a row, and they were all widowed women and they got along great. So she was happy.

Hughes: In her later years was she more feisty, like you are?

Walker: Well, she held her own.

Hughes: Tell me about this black housing area that Dianne has documented so wonderfully—Sinclair Park. Where was that from here, ladies?

Walker: It's that way (pointing west).

Hughes: I see. It was on the other side of the freeway, up past the auto dealers. So if I go up the hill toward the soccer fields and the National Guard Readiness Center, that's where it was?

Walker: Yes. That whole area up there—that's where Sinclair Park was.

Hughes: Can I interchangeably refer to it as Sinclair Park and Sinclair Heights?

Walker: Yes.

Hughes: (To Robinson) Why did you use "Park" on the history project DVD you produced?

Robinson: If you look at the Housing (Authority) papers, it was called Sinclair Park, but it's OK to say Sinclair Heights.

Walker: That is right.

Hughes: And the Postal station where you worked, Mrs. Walker, was that "Park" or "Heights"?

Walker: Well, you know I'm not sure.

Robinson: Well, I've got one of your mail things here and it says "Sinclair Heights."

Hughes: Do I understand that Sinclair Heights was, in fact, segregated housing?

Walker: There were some white people that had homes up there on the outer edge, but it, in itself, was all colored people.

Hughes: And that was by government design? Was it a government housing project?

Walker: It was a government housing project.

Hughes: If you moved to town and you were working at the Ship Yard, they just sort of steered you that way and said "You're going to live at Sinclair Heights"?

Walker: You didn't have to, but most did (because it was affordable and black families were together there). You were assigned there if they recruited you to the shipyard. There was a real sense of segregation in Bremerton. Like James and I, we moved in here, but after our kids came we were looking for a larger house. Because like I told you we started with just these four rooms. And we couldn't get a permit to add on at that point, so we got a real estate man and he came and picked us up and took us out to Navy Yard City (where a lot of black families lived).

Hughes: Where was that, Mrs. Walker?

Walker: That's down the hill from here—when you go off the freeway and you see the car lots.

Hughes: Yes.

Walker: Well, it's behind that.

Hughes: Along Sinclair Inlet there?

Walker: Yes. It was "Navy Yard City." He took us to a house. And we said, "This is not big enough." The rooms were real small, and it was worse than what we had. So, he was going to take us and show us another one. And I called him up, and I said, "Do you have a house over here on—" At that time, TB&M was up on the hill.

Hughes: What was that?

Walker: It was a grocery store. And there was a nice house down there that had a "for sale" sign on it. So we looked at it. So I called him and told him about it. "Well, that's $28,000," he said.

Hughes: Holy mackerel!

Walker: I said, "I don't remember that we gave you a price that we couldn't meet." He never did call me back.

Hughes: In other words, he was making the assumption that that was something that colored folks couldn't afford, and the wrong neighborhood.

Walker: That's right. And we called another real estate man. He lived on 5th Street. He made an appointment with us on the phone for 4 o'clock to go see that house. Well, we had a couple of friends, Marie and Jim Morris, who went with us, a white couple. You don't choose your friends by color. The real estate man got out of the car, and Marie got out, and he said, "Hi Mrs. Walker." So she said, "I'm the maid. This is Mrs. Walker." He hem-hawed. "Well, I'll go and see if we can see it." I said, "What do you mean? We had an appointment for 4 o'clock. Let's go see it." I bet he made five trips, up and back, up and back, to the house. So finally, "OK, we can see it." So all four of us went up the hill with him. He showed us the house, and we met the lady of the house. After we got through, I said, "We'll let you know whether we want it or not."

Hughes: Was James marveling at your chutzpah in putting the real estate man in his place?

Walker: Oh, he was used to it by then.

Hughes: Did he encourage you? Or did he ever take you aside and say, "Honey, we need to cool it a little bit"?

Walker: No, he never did try to talk me out of something. Because when we bought our first Chrysler, (the dealer) was down there right across from Wells Fargo Bank. So the man was quoting the price. And I said, "Well, how about—" and I was, as the saying goes, "jewing" them down. He said, "I'm the only Jew here." I said, "No you're not, I'm an adopted (Jew)." He said, "Oh!" But I never bought anything like a car, a refrigerator or anything else at full price. I tried to get them down on their price. I knew they had it priced high.

Hughes: You drive a hard bargain.

Walker: Right.

Hughes: So, you and James never really lived at Sinclair Park.

Walker: Oh no, no, no. That's why we bought this house because James and I both said, "No, we're not going up there."

Hughes: So, Dianne, how many families were up there at Sinclair Park in, say, 1943?

Robinson: 200 and some. About 200. I don't want to overdo it, but I would say about 250.

Walker: At least, yeah.

Robinson: Also, although they segregated them in Sinclair Park, they also had segregated houses in Port Orchard, called "Port Orchard Heights." They had all the blacks in that area as well. And at the college they had a dormitory where they would drop the single men in. It was called the "Duration Dormitory."

Hughes: I listened to a story on the Sinclair Park Project CD that came out in 2004. I think I'm confused about something because Mrs. Walker seemed to be telling a story about working at the shipyard. Did you actually work there?

Walker: I worked there for three months. And James was called to the NAD, Naval Ammunition Depot. So I went out and talked to Mr. Driver, his boss. And he got me transferred from the Navy Yard because I was working days and James was working swing shift.

Hughes: What were you doing at the Navy Yard?

Walker: Janitor work.

Hughes: This is before you had children though?

Walker: Oh yeah.

Hughes: And the thrust of this story I heard you telling on the Sinclair Park Project CD was that you had two ID tags at the Navy Yard, and somebody was saying you could have passed for Filipino.

Walker: The girl (in personnel) didn't know whether I was white or Filipino.

Hughes: Was the notion that if you had been labeled as a Filipino that there was less prejudice?

Walker: I doubt it.

Hughes: OK. So it was just confusion over racial identity. She didn't know how to categorize you because you were light skinned?

Walker: She gave me two cards because she didn't know which one to give me. I told her I was a Negro. That I wasn't going to wear a Filipino badge. She was stupid.

Hughes: So you only worked there at the Ship Yard for just a few months.

Walker: Just a few months until we went and talked to the boss out at the Naval Ammunition Depot and he got transferred out there.

Hughes: And were you doing the same sort of work?

Walker: Pretty much, yeah.

Hughes: With this experience that you'd had in nursing, had you thought about the medical field?

Walker: I tried to get a job at the hospital, but they wouldn't hire.

Hughes: Was that on account of race do you think?

Walker: Well, I think so. But they said wouldn't hire me because they said I didn't have a certificate (for nursing school).

Hughes: Tell me about when it was that you got this excellent job with the U.S. Postal Service. How did that come to be?

Walker: Well, they had an ad in *The Bremerton Sun*. And the class was at the main Post Office. There were seven or eight of us that took it.

Shift change at the Shipyard during World War II. *Puget Sound Naval Shipyard*

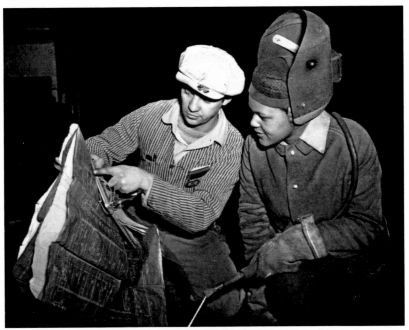

Two Shipyard welders during World War II. *Puget Sound Naval Shipyard*

Hughes: What year was that? 1942?

Walker: Yes. And so I took the test and I was the head of the class.

Hughes: The top scorer in the class?

Walker: Yes. And the postmaster (Carl S. Halverson) sent me to the West Park Post Office for training. And then after I took the training there, then they sent me off to the post office at Sinclair Park, and put me in charge there. Then after a few months I got pregnant. So I told them, "I'm going to have to quit." "Well, Mrs. Walker, you just got started." They were sorry to see me leave. I said, "I know. But I'm going to have a baby, and I'm not going to have babies for somebody else to raise. I'm going to raise my son myself, my husband and I." They said, "Well, I understand that. Can you train the lady who is helping you?" "Sure." So I trained her, and then one weekend I started having labor pains and I had to go to the hospital. So I didn't go back to work.

Hughes: Who was the lady you trained to succeed you?

Walker: I don't remember her name. She was a black lady.

Hughes: So, Sinclair Park had a black post office. Is that right?

Walker: Right.

Hughes: It's hard to believe isn't it?—the changes you've seen in your lifetime.

Robinson: I've interviewed a lot of the older people who experienced things like Mrs. Walker did. After 50 years you can go in and get all the paperwork, all the confidential files. So I went and got all the confidential files and read about everything that was said about these people.

Hughes: Concerning this "confidential report" we found from 1944 about the "Negro Situation" in Bremerton, am I right in my characterization that it was the Navy Department keeping an eye on its Negroes, to make sure they weren't going to make trouble?

Robinson: They even had a list of every African-American person here who had guns. And the neo-Nazis were here. And you know what they were? They were people who worked at the *military*.

Walker: Right.

Robinson: The neo-Nazis were here.

Hughes: They were nervous with good reason because in the L.A. area at that time black folks had gotten tired of being treated like third-class citizens. Some of those young black GI's were court martialed in a famous case for refusing to do demeaning work.

Robinson: There were cases here like that. It's really interesting to hear some of the things that went on. They thought the NAACP was a Communist Party.

Hughes: Well, I mean "those people must be commies if they think they should be treated just like white Americans."

Walker: One time a fellow worker ran his mouth and said something. James cautioned him: "Don't say that in the Navy Yard or you'll get fired." He didn't pay attention to what James said. And they fired him because they thought he was a Communist. I don't know if he ever admitted to it or not.

Hughes: He was a black man?

Walker: Oh yeah.

Robinson: There were several of them who lost their jobs.

Walker: And James tried to persuade him to not say anything about the Communist Party—not a nickel going to their party or anything.

Hughes: You know, the Communist Party U.S. did make some infiltrations into the NAACP and other civil rights groups.

Robinson: Yeah, they talked about that in the records I found. They named some of the women. I have all the NAACP records too.

Hughes: You've got a book there, you know that, Dianne?

Walker: Some of the white women were admitted communists, right?

Hughes: In the Northwest at that time, especially in Seattle, there was a lot of Leftist politics—"the Popular Front"—a lot of people of different liberal persuasions. And it was a scary time too, with the war going on. The Finns on Grays Harbor were split three ways politically—left, right and center. Meantime, (in the 1920s and '30s) the Ku Klux Klan had a *huge* number of outposts in the Northwest, and they signed up people in the military, too. It was really virulent. Oregon, of all places, rural Oregon, was a Klan hotbed. But they were opposed not only to black folks, but to Catholics, Jews, Greeks and immigrants of all stripes. The things that you've seen in your lifetime are just incredible, Mrs. Walker.

Walker: Right. It is amazing.

Robinson: Even that the guards at the (Navy Yard) gates were beating up the black guys. I mean, it's all on record.

Hughes: Were there a lot of black sailors here as well?

Walker: Oh yeah.

Hughes: Was there a separate USO club for blacks? (A United Service Organizations social club)

Robinson: Yes there was.

Walker: That was down on Burwell wasn't it?

Robinson: Yeah, 850 Burwell Street.

Hughes: Is the building still there, Dianne?

Robinson: Yes, it's a Masonic Temple, and is still there. It was incredible some of the things that went on. But I'm thinking the Northwest was no different than what was happening all over the United States, you know.

Walker: But, it was worse out here. Well, worse than in Chicago—

Robinson: I think it was as bad as it was in other places. Because, I don't know if you've heard of Rosewood, Florida. That was where I had family.

Hughes: I have. They were lynching black folks left and right in the South. And making a party out of it and taking picture postcards. It was incredible. One of the most gripping books I've ever seen is a history of lynching in the United States. I mean it is just breathtakingly chilling to think that people could be so heartlessly brutal toward a fellow human being just because of the color of their skin.

Walker: That's right.

Hughes: It's amazing.

Well, I'm going to give you a break from me for a day. Thank you so much, ladies.

End of Interview 1
June 8, 2009

LILLIAN WALKER INTERVIEW 2
June 9, 2009
(With corrections and additions from June 25 and July 8 followup interviews)

Hughes: We're back with Mrs. Lillian Walker at her home in Bremerton on 6th Street.

Walker: Yes, 3801 6th Street.

Hughes: Today I need to be certain that I get you to sign something. It's a form that says that you agree to be part of this oral history project. It's all non-profit. There's no movie rights. You get to keep those if we make you famous.

Walker: (laughing) I was talking to a friend of mine that used to work for me when I worked for the bank. She said, "You know I've been telling you all these years, you need to write a book." I said, "Arlene, I'm not a writer."

Hughes: Well, we're going to write it right here and now. I'll help you.

Walker: I told her the computer says I'm going to live to 127. But if I don't have a brain, I don't want to live.

Hughes: Well, if you die before then, they can freeze your body and wake you up when there's a cure!

Walker: Right! James and I both said if we get so sick that we have to be on life support, we don't want it. And his brother and his wife— she was real sick and they wanted to put her on life support and he said no, she didn't want that.

Hughes: You keep telling me great stuff before I have the tape rolling. I just walked in and said, "You look great." And we started talking about our bouts with cancer. When you were diagnosed with uterine cancer in 1982, you said you were feeling down one day, and Ulysses, your brother, called. What did he tell you?

Walker: He said, "Sis, you've always been a fighter. You've never lost a battle in your life. And you can win this!" Well, I'd had diphtheria three times and you weren't supposed to have it but once. If you had it more than once you were pronounced dead, almost. And I had pneumonia three times, the last time in 1951....But with the cancer, Ulysses said, "Sis, you're going to come out of this. You've got to think positive. You've got to read positive. You don't think negative. No, you're not going to die." I said, "I'm going to die one day." "Well, yeah," he said, "but this cancer is not going to kill ya." I said, "OK, thank you!" And so I started thinking about what he said. Well, I would find something positive in the Bible to read. I would read anything that I could find that was positive. And I had never been a real negative person, but when something like that hits you it makes you start thinking, "Well, is this it?" I remember that my brothers and their wives gave me a 65th anniversary. And I said, "I never thought I would live to be 65." I took my Social Security early. And the lady said, "Why are you taking it early? You're losing 20 percent." I said, "Can you assure me I'm going to live to 65?" "No," she said. "I don't have that kind of power." But I turned it around. And I kept up that positive thinking. Every time I went to Seattle and had a radiation treatment I would say, "I've got to have a milkshake." I kept my weight within two pounds of what it was when I started.

Hughes: I did that too. Every day after chemo I had a root beer milkshake.

Walker: Well, I like vanilla or banana. We'd stop and get a milkshake every day. And I had 22 of those treatments, and every day I had a milkshake. And I don't mean I had a half of one.

Hughes: No, I wanted the triple scoop!

Walker: And I pulled through.

Hughes: Tell me more about that. You were just saying that you and your husband James made a point of not going to any depressing movies.

Walker: No. If we saw a movie it couldn't be depressing. This writer I told you about who had cancer, he had stressed in his book—enjoy peaceful stuff, fun stuff. Don't do anything negative. But we would search out the movie, and if it was funny we'd go. I told James, "I do not want to see any fighting, anything that was negative." And I don't to this day. If I'm reading a book and it's negative, I'll put it down. I won't read it.

Hughes: That man was named Norman Cousins, and he wrote a book about "humor therapy." I'll dig out the name of it ("Anatomy of an Illness.") He was diagnosed with cancer. And they told him he didn't have long to live so he treated himself with laughter—"The Three Stooges"; he rented Abbott & Costello movies and Jerry Lewis & Dean Martin.

Walker: He cured himself.

Hughes: Well, there's something to it—laughter as medicine.

Walker: That's right.

Hughes: You said something yesterday that just cracked me up when we were about winding down. You said something to the effect that after you met and fell in love with James, "My mother didn't like Negroes, although she was married to one..."

Walker: She didn't. When I was getting up to the getting-married age, 18 or something like that, she said, "Don't you bring no black grandkids in here." (laughing) Because I had a boyfriend, and he was black. He was *black*. But he was nice. So we broke up. I found something wrong, you know. I didn't want to go against my parents.

Hughes: Isn't that the ultimate irony? Your mom is half black, right? Your father is half black.

Walker: Yeah.

Hughes: And she is telling you not to bring any black boyfriends home.

Walker: Well, you know, thinking back, I think the reason she did that is because her mother was married to a black man. Now, one of mom's sisters was real dark. She lived in Chicago, But, this man, I never did get the whole story about what he had done to her. But one day grandma was going to cut his head off with an ax.

Hughes: Is this the lady we have the picture of here—Elvira Allen?

Walker: No, that's dad's mother.

Hughes: OK, sorry.

Walker: I'll have to try to find a picture of my other Grandma. But she was hefty, like my mother....But that's the tale that I was told. She was going to knock him out, put him on the chopping block and cut his head off.

Hughes: Because he had been abusive to her?

Walker: He had done something to her. I don't know if he had flogged her or what. But he had done something because knowing grandma, she wouldn't take any crap. I shouldn't say she's like me. *I'm like her.*

Hughes: On the way home yesterday, I couldn't help but thinking that if it had been Lillian Allen Walker who had been told to go to the back of the bus in Montgomery, well, God bless Rosa Parks but if they would have laid a hand on you, what would have happened?

Walker: Well, I didn't carry a gun or anything. I told you when we were in Monroe, Louisiana, to see James' kin and he was standing in line to go on the bus and I said, "Honey, you've got to get me out of this town or I'll kill somebody."

Hughes: Rosa Parks was also born in 1913, by the way. What were some of the things that your parents told you when you growing up to boost your self-esteem? Did they always tell you that you were as good as anyone, or you could be anything you wanted to be?

Walker: Oh, definitely, yeah. They were definitely like that.

Hughes: What were the words that your mom or your dad would have used?

Walker: How do you mean?

Hughes: What did they say when they were educating their children about self respect and sticking up for themselves?

Walker: Well one thing, I think it was Dad who said, "You can do anything anybody else can do." Well, I always carried that. I said, "I can do anything you can do, only I can do it better." They were never negative.

Hughes: In that little town you grew up in, just down the road from Harrisburg in rural Illinois, was there any kind of stigma to the fact that your parents were of mixed race?

Walker: No. It's like the story I told you yesterday about the man who said, "We thought you were two old white people." They got that quite often, but not negatively.

Hughes: It's interesting to me about the gene pool and how children look like different people in the family—their coloring and features can be so different. When you look at Hazel and Moses, they appear a lot more white than you do.

Mrs. Walker calls her son. Hughes and James Walker Jr. talk briefly and agree to talk some more.

Hughes: What does your son do?

Walker: He got his Ph.D. He's an epidemiologist; he does a lot of research. When I told him I had cancer, he contacted the Cancer Institute back in New York or someplace, and he gave me the phone number for me to call them. And I called them. They said, "How did you get this number?" So I said, "Well, my son gave it to me." "Where is he?" And I told them. But they answered all my questions. They were dumbfounded that somebody had called them. And they gave me people in Seattle to contact. They were not negative; they were positive too.

Hughes: That's remarkable.

Walker: You said something when you were talking to James that was really amazing. Last night I called him to tell him how I had done (on the oral history) because he was interested. And I asked him if could I call him today while you were here. And you had the exact same idea.

Hughes: Absolutely. I want to talk with him some more. Tell me about your daughter, June.

Walker: June Marie.

Hughes: And what does June Marie do?

Walker: She works for the state and she babysits for her daughter. Her daughter Mandy is married to a man who works for his dad in an automobile shop. Mandy had bought a house when she was single, and then they got married. They sold the house. And they were looking for another house. I said, "OK, Mandy, when you find a house I'll give you a thousand dollars."

Hughes: This is your granddaughter?

Walker: This is my granddaughter. And so they found the house and so I sent her a check for a thousand dollars.

Hughes: Aren't you something?

Walker: Well, you know, I try to help.

Hughes: Where does June live?

Walker: She lives in Tacoma.

Hughes: (Studying the picture of Grandma Elvira Allen with a baby and a young black woman). I sure wish we knew who this beautiful young woman was.

Walker: You know, I used to know who that is.

Hughes: What's your hunch? Your hunches are really good, Mrs. Walker.

Walker: Well, my hunch…I don't know if she was a wife of one of dad's brothers. I really don't know. At one point I did know, and I keep asking the Lord, "Can you bring this woman back to me?"

Hughes: It looks like a generational photo. I would imagine it's grandma, daughter-in-law, and a grandchild.

Walker: This is the award I was awarded. (The Kitsap County Bar Association's 2009 Liberty Bell Award for promoting a better understanding of the Constitution and the Bill of Rights.)

Hughes: That's really gorgeous.

Walker: It's heavy, too.

Hughes: Judge Robin Hunt nominated you for the award.

Walker: Oh, she is amazing. I tell you, she is really so. We get to talking sometimes. You know, we are just alike. And she thinks positive. She does not think negative. We just fell in love. She's great.

Hughes: This morning, I went down across the freeway, up above the auto dealerships, up on the hill overlooking Bremerton, and there's a big soccer complex up there, and a training academy. Is that where Sinclair Park was?

Walker: That's where Sinclair Park was.

Hughes: Where the street sign says "Sinclair Way"?

Walker: Yeah. And there were houses and a church up there and a restaurant.

Hughes: Take me back, if you will, to when you arrived. I want to be sure I've got the timeline right. Was it in 1941 that James came to Seattle?

Walker: I think he arrived in Seattle in late '40.

Hughes: Late 1940?

Walker: Yes. Do you remember the first bridge coming from Tacoma that sank?

Hughes: Yes. I know about it.

Walker: Well, he was here when that sank.

Hughes: That would have been the first Tacoma Narrows Bridge, "Galloping Gertie."

Walker: "Galloping Gertie," right.

EDITOR'S NOTE: the bridge broke apart in a wind storm on November 7, 1940.

Hughes: Then Lillian arrives from Illinois early in 1941?

Walker: Yeah. Then we were in Longview, working for that couple. We came to Bremerton in June of 1941. He got his call to the Navy Yard. And so we came back to Seattle, then to Bremerton.

Hughes: Were you married in Seattle that May?

Walker: Yes, we were. Judge DeGrief, Roy DeGrief, married us. James' mother knew him. He was her attorney. I don't know why I call him "judge." I think he was a judge, but he was an attorney. And he married us.

EDITOR'S NOTE: Roy DeGrief, was a Seattle Traffic Court judge as well as a practicing attorney.

Hughes: Then James went to work at the Ship Yard.

Walker: Yes, that's where he got his interview. And then they sent him out to Jackson Park, which was a NAD—Naval Ammunition Depot at that time. That's where they stored ammunition. It was on the west side. Well, say where you come in over here on the highway. If you had gone down, straight down, you would have come into Kitsap Way. Then you turn left, and you go out there, and the hotel is out there, and the graveyard is on this side. But then I would say a mile up the hill is where you go into the NAD (Naval Ammunition Depot).

Hughes: Is that when you got a job at the Ship Yard? You were doing some janitorial work there.

Walker: Yes.

Hughes: And that's when they gave you the two ID tags, one "white" and one "Filipino"?

Walker: Two badges, yeah. She just wasn't going to put "Negro" on there. She thought she was doing me a favor. People around town would say to me, "Are you Filipino?" And I'd say, "No, I'm a Negro."

Hughes: And were they identical that they had your picture on them, but one said "Filipino" and one said "White"?

Walker: I don't think they had my picture on them. I had to turn them in when I retired from there. I never used but the one of them because I didn't want to get the girl in trouble. I didn't want to see her lose her job. And then they transferred me out to NAD (Ammunitions Depot). They had women and men and all working out there. And they had a women's restroom. Well, I was put in charge of that. (laughing) Why I'm laughing is that the toilets got plugged up.

Hughes: As toilets will.

Walker: Yeah, especially when you put Kotex in there. So, Mr. Driver, the manager, I was trying to think of his name. Anyway, he called me up and he said, "Now, if you have to stand at the door of the restroom and watch them and see that they don't put anything in there…" And there was one girl. They were all white, but me. And I told them what Mr. Driver had said. "Well, how are you going to know?" I said, "Well, if I have to stand here with the door open and watch you, I will." And one of the girls…I'm trying to remember why I said what I did to her because I said, "You're white, but you sure act like a black woman." And she said, "What do you mean?" I said, "Your attitude. You're just not nice."

Hughes: How did she process that information? Was she offended?

Walker: Well, she laughed. "Why would you say that?" I said, "Well, you don't want to do what I told you to do. And Mr. Driver said that if you didn't, then I was to stand with the door open and see what you did." But I never had any more trouble.

Hughes: So, how long did you work there between the Ship Yard and the NAD?

Walker: Oh, you know, I don't remember. I got pregnant in '43, and I said to James, "Now, I'm not going to work. I can't work and raise a baby too."

Hughes: So, you were a mom for the rest of your career.

Walker: Right. That pregnancy was with my first daughter, and I lost her. We went to Seattle and it was about two weeks before I was to deliver. I stayed with James' mother; he came on back home. And one morning I started labor pains. They took me to the doctor, and then to the hospital. And they had to deliver the baby. I was in terrible pain. And they took my blood pressure, and the last I saw my blood pressure was 173, and I knew that was really high. And when I came to they had delivered the baby, and the baby was dead. And so the next morning I was complaining to the doctor that my stomach was hurting. And he said, "You better be glad you're alive. We had to fight to save you." I said, "OK." Ok, I'm alive, I lived through it. Then I got pregnant with Jimmy in '45. And he was born

August 29, 1945.

Hughes: Was James a healthy baby?

Walker: He was healthy. It was the happiest day of my life. And he was born down here at the hospital in Bremerton. So one morning the nurse came in and brought this beautiful little boy in—black hair—and she said, "I don't believe this is your baby." I said, "Let me see. This is my *baby*." They kept me in the hospital for about 10 days.

Hughes: Why didn't they believe it was your baby?

Walker: He was so light.

Hughes: But James, his father is darker skinned.

Walker: Yeah, but he was light. He was real light. He may be a little shade darker than me, not much. His picture is here on the table. But anyway, they let me out of the hospital. Nine days, I was sitting on the side of the bed, I said, "How come I can't go home?" "Well, the doctor doesn't want you to go home this soon." I said, "My Lord, I only had a baby." But anyway, that's when the doctor said "no more." And so that's when they

James, Lillian and Jimmy in the 1940s

went in (and tied my tubes). The doctor also said, "How come you didn't tell me you had appendicitis?" I said, "I've had appendicitis ever since I worked in the hospital. back in Illinois. The doctor would put me to bed, and keep ice packs on me. He didn't want to do the operation because I couldn't work if I had an operation, you know."

Hughes: That's back when you were the doctor's assistant.

Walker: Yes, right.

Hughes: You had appendicitis for all that time?

Walker: One day I was in Seattle and I had an appendicitis attack, but I knew how to take care of it, you know, put some ice on it and lay down and be quiet.

Hughes: Did they remove your appendix after you had James and had your tubes tied?

Walker: Yes. I said, "Well, since you found that it was bad, did you remove it?" "Yes!" he said.

Hughes: "As long as I'm in that neighborhood!"

Walker: Right. So, that's why no more children.

Hughes: So, let's go back to when you arrived here in Bremerton. Did you run into instances of racism right away? The "We cater to white trade only" signs?

Walker: Oh, those signs were in the windows of most every restaurant. And like I told you about the restaurant we were in on Burwell Street.

Hughes: Burwell?

Walker: Yes, its downtown, just off of Pacific. We didn't pay any attention to them because we had never run into anything like that.

Hughes: And when you met other people of color, did they say—

Walker: Nobody had ever said anything about it.

Hughes: They were just going along with it?

Walker: But I said, "Well, I've never been discriminated like this in my life." We had two black school teachers, and there was a restaurant down here on the highway. I almost thought of the name of it. And all the teachers, the white teachers and these two colored women, would go there for lunch. They went in one day for lunch and the manager wasn't going to seat the colored teachers, Lillian Mitchell and Orie Green, in with the other teachers. The white teachers said, "Well, we won't eat here if you're not going to serve everybody." And so, that's another red flag gone up for me. Now, what's going on here in this town? Those women, they were not derogatory. They just wanted to eat lunch. I just couldn't understand why you're serving food and why you would cut back on your profits by not serving someone.

Hughes: Absolutely. When you formed the NAACP chapter, who else was there at the beginning?

Walker: Al and Hazel Colvin and I think the Murphys were here at that time. And Mr. and Mrs. Simmons. And we got the required number because we worked through Olympia, and we worked through Seattle. I think we had to have 50 people on the charter. And Dianne Robinson, I imagine, has a copy of that charter.

Hughes: But there hadn't been an NAACP Chapter here before?

Walker: Oh no, not here.

Hughes: Did you get solid help from the Olympia and Seattle branches?

Walker: Oh yeah. That's how we got it set up.

Hughes: And the attorney, Charles Stokes, who came to town for your civil rights meeting in 1944 when the Navy was watching you—was he a good stalwart for the cause?

Walker: Oh yes.

Hughes: I keep thinking that I know that name. I think he became a judge. Did he have some really famous cases, Mr. Stokes?

Walker: Well, as far as we were concerned, we think so.

EDITOR'S NOTE: Charles Moorehead Stokes (1903-1996) in 1950 became the second black member of the Legislature in state history and in 1968 became the first black District Court judge in King County History.

Hughes: Tell me about this mass meeting here that took place on February 20, 1944, where you placed a notice in the newspaper. It said, "All Negroes interested in peaceful and legal ways of getting rid of 'We cater to white trade only' signs are encouraged to attend....Attorney C.M. Stokes, speaker, sponsored by the Puget Sound Civic Society."

Walker: That was a group that was organized (to fight racism). We had to have help. We couldn't do it alone. We wanted something with some backbone.

Hughes: William Simmons was the secretary/treasurer of the Civic Society, and Thomas Wood was the vice-president.

Walker: Yeah. He and his wife lived here at that time.

Hughes: Robert D. Addison was the president.

Walker: Addison was with the Housing Authority.

Hughes: These are all black folks?

Walker: So far.

Hughes: And John Dillon was the sergeant at arms.

Walker: He lived up in Sinclair Heights, he and his family.

Hughes: So, at the same time as you were working with the NAACP you were also members of the Puget Sound Civic Society?

Walker: We worked in anything that we could get to get a foothold and to put a stop to this racism.

Hughes: So, James, your husband, was every bit as active in the NAACP as you were?

Walker: Yeah, I think I'm more outspoken, but he backed me up. We backed each other up in whatever. Like we were at a meeting one night and one of the colored men—Frank Giggans, if I remember right—said something to this Caucasian lady who was with me. I have been trying to rack my brain to remember her name. And they were discussing something on race, and so Frank got up and said, "And why did you come here?" to the white lady. I got up and said, "She came with me. I brought her here because she's a friend." I believe she was a member of the NAACP. Well, that quieted that.

Hughes: It's not surprising to me, but it's really heartening that you're such a colorblind person. You just like people.

Walker: I like people. I don't care what color you are, if you are for the right. If you're a bad white man, you're a rat. Just like a bad black person.

Hughes: A rat is a rat is a rat.

Walker: That's right. We had one family in Illinois not too far from where we lived. They were Negroes, but as far as I'm concerned they were niggers.

Hughes: Sort of like the equivalent of "white trash"?

Walker: That's right, that's right, yeah. Some of the kids were almost as white as I am. The mother and the father were colored. They were like my parents. But they didn't believe like we did. And the boys were always in trouble. So, anyway, like I said before if somebody says, "That's a nigger," I say, "Well, what color are they?" "What difference does that make?" I said, "It makes a lot of difference."

Hughes: That brings them up short, doesn't it?

Walker: It sure does, yeah.

Hughes: So tell me more about the barber shop incident where the fellow said he'd cut James' hair with the shades pulled.

Walker: That was down on Callow.

Hughes: On Callow Avenue?

Walker: Yeah. The main street in West Bremerton.

Hughes: About what year was that?

Walker: That was probably in '42 because we were living down at the Simmons Apartments down on South Callow, 222-1/2 South Callow.

Hughes: With any of these incidents, apart from some threats, were there ever any real standoffs—where real menacing white people came up and said …

Walker: No. They just come to your table and tell you that "we can't serve you."

Hughes: Did you stage any kind of sit-ins?

Walker: Well, we had something like that, including stand-outsides.

Busy Farragut Avenue during World War II. *Puget Sound Navy Museum*

And we had a march once from the Post Office to downtown.

Hughes: About what year was that?

Walker: That was probably within the year of Martin Luther King marching in the South.

Hughes: So this is in the '60s?

Walker: Yes. And we marched from the Post Office, which is on 6th and Pacific, and we marched down into town.

Hughes: But there weren't instances involving James and Lillian and friends where you refused to leave a place?

Walker: No.

Hughes: You left, regrouped and took legal action.

Walker: That's right. We wanted it done legal. We didn't want it to be a personal. We wanted the legal action.

Hughes: Have you thought some more about some of the Caucasian folks who were helping you make a difference, who were really courageous?

Walker: Well, you know, Peggy Gustafson was one. She and I and some of the other members of the NAACP went across the street to the restaurant near the YMCA. And Art Morken, the chief of police, came down to investigate claims of racism. Peggy and I worked together.

Hughes: I went to see Adele Ferguson after I left here yesterday.

Walker: Oh, did you?

Hughes: And she was just delighted that I had been talking to you. And she said something really lovely. She said, "You know, Lillian and James Walker and the other black folks who came to Bremerton were all first-rate folks."

Walker: Well, bless her heart.

Hughes: We skipped over something yesterday. I always try to ask people about where they were and what their reaction was to major events in their lives. So let me ask you about December 7, 1941, "a date which will live in infamy."

Walker: I can remember that day.

Hughes: Tell me about it.

Walker: I had worked that night, and of course I came home and went to bed. The next morning, when I started waking up, well, James said, "Honey, we're in war." Well, I didn't grasp it right away. I went, "What do you mean?" "Well," he said, "the United States is in war." And he thought for sure he was going to have to go in the service. But they refused him. They made him an F...

Hughes: 4F?

Walker: 4F. I guess they thought he didn't have the stamina. I don't know. But he was 4F.

Hughes: He was doing some pretty essential war work (at the shipyard).

Walker: Oh, he was.

Hughes: What was James' job by then?

Walker: He was in electricity. He worked in electronics.

Hughes: He took a lot of courses to get himself educated?

Walker: Oh, he did. He took correspondence courses. He went to Olympic College and took the electrical course there. He always had his nose in a book. He studied. He became an inspector of the electronics on the ships.

Workers stream off a ship to celebrate victory over Japan in 1945.
Kitsap County Historical Society Museum

Hughes: During World War II, there was a lot of concern on the West Coast that the Japanese might try to stage an invasion and that there were Japanese submarines off the coast. Do you remember a real sense of anxiety or heightened awareness of that danger?

Walker: Yes, because one time we were having…everybody was in their cars headed out of town.

Hughes: An evacuation?

Walker: Well, similar to an evacuation, and I said to James, "Well, if the Japanese is going to strike, they know when to strike because they'll kill all of us! And the next time the city calls this…I'm not going to get in the car because for miles you were backed up.

Hughes: What were they having you do? Was it some sort of drill?

Walker: Yes. A drill, I believe. But I told James in the car, "I will not be in another one of these! I'm gonna stay home, even if I have to hide!"

Hughes: Did you have blackout kind of drills, too?

Walker: Oh yeah. You had black shades you pulled down so no light went out.

Hughes: On the home front, this is where it was all happening: Building ships, repairing ships and getting them back in the fight. Boeing's building B-17s. You know there were some incidents that didn't get a lot of notoriety at the time, but the Japanese actually put bombs onto balloons and drifted them over the West Coast.

Walker: I didn't hear that!

Hughes: But here in Bremerton there was this palpable feeling that you were at war?

Walker: Oh yeah. And we thought, "Well, if they want to bomb Kitsap County there's no place we can hide, even though we had a cellar, with two walls of concrete, so we could go there. We were very aware of our circumstances being at a Navy Yard and what we might encounter.

Hughes: Did James retire from the Naval shipyard?

Walker: He worked there for 30 years total. In 1968 they laid him off. And he went to Seattle. He had worked at a clothing store there, and they hired him back. He would take the ferry and go to work in the clothing store. Meanwhile, he'd be looking for a better job. We thought we were going to have to move to Seattle. I worked in the theater (as a custodian), and I kept that going.

Hughes: The same theater as earlier?

Walker: The Tower Theater on 4th Street.

Hughes: And you were doing janitorial things there?

Walker: That's right. James went to Boeing and applied for a job, but they wouldn't hire him, even though they knew he had worked at the Navy Yard. But within two weeks he was hired back to the Navy Yard. And then he worked there for nearly 30 years in all. Until one day—I think it was on a Friday—they came to him and told him, "As of 4 o'clock today you will no longer be an employee." He said, "OK." He got on the phone and called Boeing's and a Seattle company (Lockheed Shipbuilding Co. on Harbor Island) that was doing work for the Navy. He called a lady (in personnel) that he had met someplace and told her what had happened. She said, "Can you come to work Monday morning?" He said, "I'll be there!" Then at 4 o'clock his boss at the (Bremerton) shipyard came back and said, "We have decided to keep you on." And James said, "Well, I'm sorry to tell you, but I go to work in Seattle Monday morning." The boss said, "What do you mean?!" And James said, "Well, I got a job in Seattle." "Well, how did you do that?" Knowing James, he wouldn't tell them all the details. He just said, "I called someone I know, and they asked me if I'd come to work Monday morning, and I promised that I would. So I can't stay here. I gave my word I'd be to work Monday morning. And I plan to do that." It was shocking that they would treat him like that. In the long run, he found out that Boeing had called the Navy Yard asking about him and that's why they called him back in and said he still had a job. He lacked two weeks of having 30 years. But he worked over there in Seattle for the "Soup" (the Navy's Superintendent of Shipbuilding) as an electrical inspector for about eight years. He had 39 years in government work when he retired. The Seattle job was still on his records.

Hughes: It counted for his pension?

Walker: Yes, that's right.

Hughes: OK, do you think the layoffs were tinged with racism?

Walker: I would bet my last dollar on it.

Hughes: Still persisting after all those years. But when you won the case against the drug store owner in 1954 did you feel that you were really making some noise, getting noticed, making progress—"these signs are coming down"?

Walker: Yes. But we were making some progress in the 1940s. We just went on living our lives and if we felt like one night, let's go have a hamburger or let's go have dinner or something, we could and we did.

Hughes: The "We cater to whites only" signs were down (by 1954)?

Walker: Yes. "We reserve the right to refuse service to anyone." They didn't say "No Negroes Wanted."

Hughes: In the beginning, though, did they say "We cater to white

James Walker receiving his 35-year pin in 1977.

trade only"? Because in this ad the civil rights group placed that's what it says the signs said.

Walker: Yeah. That's right.

Hughes: But then later they got more subtle and they said, "We reserve the right ..."

Walker: Right.

Hughes: Sort of like that "No shoes, no shirt, no service," thing?

Walker: That's right. But we felt that we were moving forward. At least we had moved off of the signs. But there were other issues, like the paper would not print a Negro picture on the front of the paper unless he had committed some terrible crime, like raping a woman or killing someone. So we broke that up. Do you know Gene Gisley?

Hughes: I did know Gene Gisley, the longtime editor of *The Bremerton Sun.* Was he a good man in your view?

Walker: *Oh,* he was!

Hughes: I'm glad to hear that because I always liked Gene.

Walker: He was a good man.

Hughes: I was sorry when he retired from *The Sun*.

Walker: He was *really* a good guy. You know, if we went down to the paper, we could either talk to him or Adele. And we knew that we were going to get what we wanted.

Hughes: But before that more humanistic group of people arrived at the Bremerton newspapers, if you got engaged or married and you happened to be black folks they weren't going to put your picture in the paper? Is that the way it went?

Walker: No, you definitely didn't make the paper. If you had done some horrible crime, then your picture would be on the front page.

Hughes: You're a founding member—a charter member—of the Bremerton YWCA. Tell me all about that. What year are we talking about now?

Walker: I think either '47 or '48, I believe, something like that. But this lady came to me, Dotsy Fine, she …

Hughes: Tell me her name again, Mrs. Walker.

Walker: Dotsy Fine—Dorothy Fine. She was from Texas. And oh she was a jewel. She and I worked together on the PTA and the YWCA. My son Jimmy and her daughter were going to Hillcrest Kindergarten School. We met and we worked together in the PTA. And we worked together on that. Then later on we worked through high school, the PTA. Dotsy and I became good friends. And she said, "We're trying to get a group together to form the YWCA. Would you join?" I said, "Sure. If you're in it, I know it's something (worthwhile)." And that's how I became interested in the YWCA.

Hughes: And was there a need for the Young Women's Christian Association as well as a YMCA? I assume Bremerton had a YMCA, too?

Walker: Yeah. But there was no place to speak of for women.

Hughes: Women of any color?

Walker: Oh yeah. We worked through the Tacoma YWCA. At one time I worked in Tacoma for a company that had built apartment houses and

Lillian surrounded by admirers at the YWCA's 60th anniversary celebration.

they wanted people (as tenants). And I was calling on groups of people and persons on a list they would give me, and I would go and tell them they could get an apartment in this apartment house with their Social Security.

Hughes: Sure, you're helping people find affordable housing.

Walker: Yes, helping people. And I called on the YWCA to see if they had people that needed an apartment, so I could direct them where to go.

Hughes: I read that the Bremer Trust, from the original founder of Bremerton, gave a gift to the YWCA to get it started.

Walker: This is right.

Hughes: And it opened with a lounge and a hotplate in 1948 and coffee was 5 cents a cup, if you could afford it?

Walker: That's right, and if you couldn't afford it, you got it anyway. It was on Second Street before you get to Pacific and just a couple of doors off of Washington.

Hughes: Is the YWCA still going strong in Bremerton?

Walker: Oh yeah.

Hughes: In the beginning, did it offer all the classic things, like recreational activities and temporary lodging?

Walker: Right. They had a house off of 6th Street onto Highland. The man had died and the widow had the privilege of living there until her death, and that was given to the YWCA. So that was our headquarters. And then years later they turned that into a house for families.

Hughes: A halfway house?

Walker: That's right, a halfway house.

Hughes: Like a shelter for women, victims of domestic violence?

Walker: Right. And kids, too, because a lot of these women have kids and they had nowhere to go. Before that, women had come over from Seattle or somewhere and they didn't have any place to stay. So we would rent them a room for the night.

Hughes: Where did you get the rest of the funds to start the YWCA? Did you have fundraising events?

Walker: Yes. We'd have different affairs, fundraisers, you know.

Hughes: Bake sales and rummage sales?

Walker: Oh yeah. We had bake sales, we had rummage sales, and in that house we could put on lunches. So we would have lunches and people from all over town would come to them. So we had different things to raise money.

Hughes: Has Congressman Norm Dicks been a good friend over the years?

Walker: Oh, you can't beat Norm Dicks. Like, last year we had the 60th year anniversary of the Y, and he was there. He came and he sat by me. We were talking politics and Norm said, "Can I count on your vote?" I said, "You know better than that. We have supported you—James and I—we have supported you from the beginning. You better not back out now." He's a good friend.

Hughes: How about mayors over the years. Who have been supportive of civil rights and other civic programs?

Walker: Some of them. We had one problem with a mayor in getting him on board with the YWCA.

Hughes: What year was that? Was that "Whitey" Domstad?

Walker: That was him. We finally turned him around and he agreed to talk with us, you know.

Hughes: Turned him around—good for you.

Walker: Yeah. Then he was more on our side, so to speak, with the YWCA. Then we had Mayor (Glenn) Jarstad. His secretary called me (one time) and said that "Mayor Jarstad wants to appoint you as a trustee on the …"—let me get this right now—"on the Library Board of Trustees." And I said, "I have one question. I can speak to him, or you can ask him." I said, "Can I use my brain? Can I speak freely of what I believe?" And so he came on the phone. He said, "I wouldn't have it any other way." I said, "OK. I will accept." He appointed me to the Library Board of Trustees. And it worked out fine. I really enjoyed that!

Hughes: That must have been fun for you since you love books so much.

Walker: Well, it was fun, but it was work. And it was *needed* work.

Hughes: What were some of the things you did, Mrs. Walker, to improve the Bremerton Library?

Walker: We went around, all over the state, looking at furniture. We were going to build a new one. We started in from the ground up. We got this property. And that's one thing I'm really proud of in Bremerton. I say, "I was on the ground floor of getting that branch started." It's on the east side, on Sylvan Way. We got the property and then we hired an architect to design the building. All of us who were on the board had input in that. We went all over the state looking at libraries because we had to furnish it. Then when they started the building we had this berm and they were going to put ivy on it. There was a lady from Kingston on the board. She and I were the only ones who put our foot down. *No ivy* because it will come in and it will eat up the building. It will kill a tree. So we stood firm on that.

Hughes: You're a longtime Garden Club member, too. You really know your plants, don't you?

Walker: I knew enough because I had seen this ivy. It will kill trees. And she and I both said the same thing.

Hughes: It's pretty, but it will damage concrete too.

The annual tea of the Carver Civic Club in 1966. Hazel Colvin is at left,
Mrs. Walker third from left, and Gert Joseph fifth from left.

Walker: So it's in the contract that the ivy would never be allowed to touch the walls of the library.

Hughes: What year did you open that branch?

Walker: I don't recall. But I was on there, I think, for five years or something like that.

Hughes: Well, you helped found a new YWCA, and that's a pretty remarkable achievement all by itself. You got the "whites only" signs taken down. You made some real headway in the 1940s. After the war, was the population of Bremerton, in terms of demographics, pretty much about the same?

Walker: After the war it went down.

Hughes: In terms of?

Walker: Of people.

Hughes: People all told—people of all creeds and colors?

Walker: Yes, all told because some people came to Bremerton for the duration of the war. And so, like the Greers, they had planned to go back to Kansas. But things changed. He got a job in the Navy Yard. We came to Bremerton to live. We didn't come here for a duration, you know. But a lot of people came here, and as soon as the war was over they were ready to go.

Hughes: Were there a lot fewer black people here after the war?

Walker: Oh yes. A lot fewer. A lot of them said, "I want to get out of this place as soon as I can," and I said, "You should stay and make a place likable." That was always my policy. But hundreds left. Even though they established two other black churches, Mount Zion Missionary Baptist and Sinclair Missionary Baptist. The "missionary" part denotes working to help people—being a missionary.

Hughes: Did you ever get to a point in that struggle for civil rights that you and James and those other folks who helped were discouraged, and you thought, "Boy, we're going to have to leave this place"?

Walker: You know, when you're fighting for something, you don't give up. You wait. You're going to get the top or die trying.

Hughes: Well, it's a nice place to live, too, isn't it, right on Puget Sound?

Walker: I think so. A lot of people didn't like Bremerton, but I don't mind. I like Bremerton.

Hughes: What's the main difference in the town today, other than the fact that it's a lot more welcoming place? When I was in high school at Aberdeen in the early 1960s we had football games against Bremerton schools. We always knew that it was the same sort of place as Aberdeen/Hoquiam, that it would be a tough game. In fact, there were a couple of famous Aberdeen-Bremerton football games in the 1960s. Bremerton had a great running back named Steve Bramwell.

Walker: I remember him.

Hughes: He was fast. And there was this real rivalry. But, what's the difference in the town today? Is Bremerton a far different place from when you arrived in the early 1940s?

Walker: Oh, it's a far different place because we had a lot of stores, like Bremer's, which was a real nice store, JC Penney, Woolworth. And then we had a nice restaurant down on the end of Pacific, before you go in the Navy Yard, a real nice restaurant there. You really thought you were top dollar if you went in there.

Hughes: What was the name of that place?

Walker: I don't remember.

Hughes: So, the downtown just got decimated in the '60s?

Walker: Well, it did get worn down. And finally there were several famous stores on Pacific. And the bank that started up on 2nd and Pacific.

Hughes: So, something was happening downtown.

Walker: There's always been something happening downtown. I remember one time we went to a meeting down on the lower Pacific before you get to 1st Street, and the meeting was upstairs. I said, "Oh, we're going up to the whorehouse," because it used to be a whorehouse.

Hughes: Back in the '40s and '50s Bremerton was still a pretty wide open town, wasn't it?

Walker: Oh yeah!

Hughes: So, there were a lot of tattoo parlors and saloons and houses of ill repute.

Walker: Especially that, yes, right.

Hughes: Not that you would know!

Walker: Well, one time I worked at one. I was the housekeeper, you know, and served the girls coffee or tea.

Hughes: In Aberdeen, where I grew up, one theory was that the "tolerance" policy toward prostitution kept the women folks safe from the rampaging loggers, sailors and all that element.

Walker: That's right. There were a lot of whorehouses downtown in Bremerton. Some people were talking one day about that. And I said, "Well, I work in that one!"

Hughes: Which one was that?

Walker: Lord, I don't remember the name. (chuckling) People would say, "You were a *whore*?" I said, *"No, I wasn't a whore."*

Hughes: (Laughing) I think it's amazing that this woman with such strong morals and such dignity—

Walker: Worked in a whorehouse!

Hughes: You were a *custodian.*

Walker: That's right.

Hughes: How long did you work there?

Walker: Oh, a couple of years. Down on Pacific between 2nd and 1st Street. So, one day we were getting the laundry ready to go. And the madam, she's down here with these towels at her nose. I said, "Don't you want some gloves on?" And she said, "No." And I said, "Well, I'm not going to handle those towels." These are towels the women had used. I said, "I'm not handling those towels without my gloves on."

Hughes: So, you were handling the linens?

Walker: The linens. Well, we called them "Tail towels" because that's what they were.

Hughes: "Tail towels." I've never heard that one! That's great!…So, back in the 1940s and 1950s as you're making the headway on civil rights, did you ever have any problems, really, with the schools?

Walker: No. The only problem I had, and I think I told you about that yesterday, was when I brought my brother Ulysses out here and I had to warn his teacher about racist language.

Hughes: Did she get it right away, do you think, when you upbraided her?

Walker: She didn't do it again.

Hughes: But did you see the look in her eyes where she thought, "My gosh, this lady just called me out on being a racist."

Walker: Well, I don't know what she thought. It was, "Yes, Mrs. Walker."

Hughes: So she wasn't patronizing to you?

Walker: No. And that was it.

Hughes: So, when would that have been?

Walker: It was '43. Yeah, 1943, because Ulysses came out here. We had gone back home and he wanted to come out here for a year. And mom and dad said, "OK, you can go. But, you've got to send him back in a year." "OK, mom." So, we sent him back. We kept our word. And he got back home and he said, "I'm going to get me a job. I'm coming back."

Hughes: Ulysses must have had cultural shock leaving the wide spot in the road in rural Illinois to come to Bremerton.

Walker: That's right. And he said, "Sis, I'm coming back." I said, "OK, tell mom and dad. See what they say."

Hughes: Bremerton must have been a happening place in World War II in terms of people.

Walker: *Oh Lord,* there were a lot of people here when we came over. A lot of people. People sleeping in the parks. I used to tell James, "We moved to Bremerton in a shopping bag." But we found the room with Nannie Jones.

Hughes: Nannie Jones?

Walker: Nannie Jones, yeah. A black lady. She had a house on 8th Street. There was a real shortage of housing during the war years—people even living in their cars, anyplace you could lay your head. I'm sure thankful that we had a decent place to stay. We rented one room. We had to go downstairs to go to the bathroom.

Hughes: She took in roomers, lodgers?

Walker: Yeah, and then she had two daughters. I forget what Nannie did. But anyway, she was a member of my church at that time.

Hughes: Have you always gone to the A.M.E. church?

Walker: Yes. Ever since I've been here. When I first came to Bremerton there were no organized Baptist churches. We had been Baptists. Well, there was a church group that met upstairs over a clothing store in downtown Bremerton. We went there one night and we didn't like what we saw.

Hughes: What didn't you like?

Walker: It was more like the Holy Sanctified to me.

Hughes: It was more of a "Holy Roller" kind of thing, to use that old phrase.

Walker: Right. I'm not a shouter. One time I told our pastor that if he heard me shouting, he'd know "that lady just lost her mind!" So, we met Mr. and Mrs. Simmons, and they invited us to their church.

Hughes: That's the same gentleman who was part of your Puget Sound Civic Society civil rights group?

Walker: Yes.

Hughes: Would the notion have been that the NAACP, by that name, would have been a more inflammatory thing than the "Puget Sound Civic Society"? That someone would have thought that the colored folks in Bremerton were making more trouble if they were packaged as the NAACP—more of a threat?

Walker: The NAACP was known to be fighting for the rights.

Hughes: Even the Navy Intelligence people say that the Puget Sound Civic Society emphasized that it wanted peaceful and orderly ways to integrate. The Navy investigators interviewed Robert D. Addison, the president of the Society, who worked at the shipyard. He "stated that from his observations, the majority of the Negros are highly dissatisfied and very much disillusioned because of existing discrimination." Then there's this wonderful line: "He pointed out that these colored workers have come here at the request of the government, and the majority of them feel the government should make a greater effort to make conditions more pleasant."

Robinson: Even the housing wasn't what it should have been. They didn't have a place to go and eat. They were discriminated against in many ways.

Walker: That's right!

Hughes: Charles M. Stokes, the civil rights attorney who spoke at that mass meeting in 1944, said it was "morale sabotage." Discrimination was sabotaging the morale of the war workers at the shipyard.

Walker: I wouldn't have used those words. I would just tell it what it was.

Hughes: What would you have said?

Walker: I said, "There is discrimination against Negros! They don't want us to have the same things they were having."

Hughes: I've seen several references to the Bremerton branch of the NAACP helping the Seattle group push through tougher anti-discrimination laws, especially the Greers and you and James.

Walker: We did. There was not one on the books in Olympia. The Bremerton unit and Seattle worked on this law. We had good attorneys to help …

Hughes: Was Mr. Stokes probably in the picture on that effort?

Walker: That's right, together with Mr. Burton.

Hughes: Were things a lot better here through the 1950s? Then came the landmark U.S. Supreme Court decision on school desegregation and things heated up in the South.

Walker: I think things gradually improved here as far as race relations—and after we sued the drug store man. But there were major problems in the South especially.

Hughes: And then in the crucible of the 1960s when Martin Luther King and the Reverend Abernathy were conducting marches and they were having police dogs sic'd on them, and fire hoses turned on them. What was it like here then? That footage is still just incredible to me.

Walker: Yeah, me too.

Hughes: And those four little girls blown to bits in Birmingham in 1963—my God, these darling little girls!

Walker: You know, at that time my son Jimmy was in Stanford and they were having voter registration down South. And he wanted to go down and work there. I said, "Oh no you don't!" I said, "We're not sending you to college to go down South. Those people run their own program. No." Because I couldn't forget that Emmett Till had gotten murdered down there (in Mississippi in 1955 for allegedly flirting with a white woman).

Hughes: The lonesome death of Emmett Till.

Robinson: Now that was the first time that I, as a young girl, really knew about discrimination. That was my first exposure to that kind of hate. My mother showed me that in a *Jet* magazine—the photos of his mutilated body. And everybody in our neighborhood could tell you about Emmett Till.

Hughes: That was an incredibly principled and gutty thing for *Jet* magazine to do, to graphically show what they'd done to that man.

Robinson: Beautiful young man.

Hughes: I remember being in Memphis, Tennessee, in 1963 when it was the absolute epitome of Southern segregated society. And I went back there for a newspaper conference in the 1990s. I stayed at the Peabody

Hotel, and I went into the restaurant there on a Sunday morning. There were black families coming back from church with their children, dressed to the nines, eating Sunday breakfast at that big hotel. I've got gooseflesh right now just thinking about how much things had changed in those 30 years. So, what happened in Bremerton in that era, Mrs. Walker? You said there was a march in the 1960s to support Dr. King's efforts?

Walker: A group of us marched from the Post Office on 6th Street and marched downtown. It was around the same time that Martin Luther King was leading a march. I don't know whether it was the same day. But there were no disturbances or anything.

Hughes: And that was people of all creeds and colors?

Walker: *All* creeds and colors.

Hughes: Were you here then, Dianne?

Robinson: Yes, I was. But I don't think I was in that march. (Addressing Mrs. Walker) I remember you guys left from the church. Or that your church was involved in that.

Walker: Yeah, our church was involved.

Robinson: There were a lot of things going on when I got here in the '60s. A lot of things were being done to her church. The Ebenezer A.M.E. Church was the most active, I think, in the community.

Walker: Oh yeah, it was.

Robinson: After I got here in '66, we did establish a group called Black Concerned Citizens. We initiated bringing black, African-American teachers here. There were practically no African-American teachers—you know, like one or two. It wasn't even that.

Hughes: When you arrived, what was the African-American population of Kitsap County? What would you say?

Robinson: I would say maybe about two percent.

Walker: That's what I was thinking.

Hughes: About 1,500 black people? 2,000?

Robinson: Yeah, I would say maybe 2,000.

Hughes: These numbers have been fairly consistent, apart from the peak during the war time, haven't they?

Robinson: I think the military has a lot to do with it. You know, the transient people. I don't know whether you would consider them as part of the population or what. A lot of military families came here during that period of time. There were three Navy ships here at one time in the 1960s.

Hughes: How about today? Is the black population still about the same today?

Robinson: No, I think it's about three percent now.

Walker: Oh, is it?

Hughes: Is that all people of color or just African-American?

Robinson: Just African American. It might be higher than that, from the 2000 census it was about three percent.

Walker: Oh really?

Hughes: How does that compare to Pierce County? Is Pierce a lot blacker than Kitsap?

Robinson: Yes, much more.

EDITOR'S NOTE: For 2008, the State Office of Financial Management extrapolated Census data and other data and estimated the population of Kitsap County at 246,800, of which 8,065 were blacks, or 3.3 percent. The 2008 estimate for Pierce County was 805,400, with 61,286 blacks, or 7.6 percent.

Hughes: By the '60s, did you have a more sophisticated, more color blind society in Bremerton because of what you'd done, Mrs. Walker?

Walker: It's really hard to say. But, yes, we'd made progress. And we've had colored people working on the (Election Day) polls. I worked on the polls. So that made a difference in getting people involved.

Hughes: You've been really active in the Democratic Party here for years, haven't you?

Walker: Oh yeah. I didn't go in to sit down and listen.

Hughes: Tell me about that. When did you first start getting active in the party?

Walker: Lord have mercy!

Hughes: Was it right from the get-go?

Walker: I'm trying to think. The 1940s. Mrs. Marie Greer asked me would I like to join, and I said yes I would. She was head of the Democratic Party for a long time.

Hughes: Was she a Caucasian lady or a person of color?

Walker: She was a person of color.

Robinson: Those two women were something else!

Walker: They called us the twins. (laughing)

Hughes: Oh, I think I saw a picture of you two.

Walker: They called us the twins wherever we went. They'd say, "Where's your twin?"

One time Marie was president of the Kitsap County Democratic Women's Club, and I was the secretary. And we worked at it. We didn't go in it just to be in something.

Hughes: Were you working hard to get young people signed up – people of all ages signed up to vote?

Walker: Trying to. We even had speakers to come to our church.

Hughes: Anybody famous?

Walker: Lord, I shouldn't have brought it up. I don't know. Jesse Jackson.

Hughes: I met Jesse Jackson on Grays Harbor in the 1970s.

Walker: Oh really?

Hughes: And that was really interesting. I was struck that he's a big man. I mean he's a big athletic guy.

Walker: Yeah, right.

Robinson: He used to come here quite often.

Walker: He sure did.

Robinson: He and Dr. McKinney came here.

Walker: Yeah, Reverend McKinney.

EDITOR'S NOTE: Samuel B. McKinney grew up in Cleveland in the 1920s and 1930s, the son of a prominent and politically engaged black minister. He attended Morehouse college, where was a classmate of the Rev. Martin Luther King Jr. McKinney moved to Seattle in 1958 to lead one of Seattle's oldest and most prominent black churches, Mt. Zion Baptist Church. McKinney quickly became a leader in the "movement for human rights," which included playing a major role in the Central Area Civil Rights Committee. McKinney retired from Mt. Zion in 1998, after serving its congregation for 40 years. But in 2005, he returned to once again lead the church that has been so instrumental in Seattle's civil rights struggles.

—UW Civil Rights and Labor History Project: http://depts.washington. edu/civilr/mckinney.htm

Hughes: Did you ever meet Jesse, Mrs. Walker?

Walker: I don't think I ever did. But James and I when we went to New York when our son was there, we got to meet Roy Wilkins, the great civil rights leader.

Robinson: Roy Wilkins came here too.

Walker: Yeah, he came here. He was a dignified person. He was great, I thought.

Hughes: What year was that Mrs. Walker?

Walker: '68.

Hughes: 1968. And what were you doing there in New York?

Walker: Our son was in school there.

Hughes: Is this after Stanford?

Walker: Yes. And he took us to see Roy Wilkins. Later, Jimmy started assistant teaching and going to school. He went to Columbia University. And then he had applied in Michigan to get his Ph.D. And when he got his offer, he took it to his counselor. And he said, "Grab it. You can't get

James Walker Jr. as a high school student.

anything," because he got a stipend as well as working on his Ph.D.

Hughes: What an achievement. You know when I think about your life, and the nearly 96 years of living you've done, it's amazing. When I was driving home, I was thinking, This lady grows up "dirt poor," as you put it, at this wide spot in the road. She ploughs the earth and she's plunking squirrels and rabbits. It's an amazing story to see what you and James did with your lives, how you changed things and raised these kids, particularly this son with a Ph.D. in epidemiology. That must make you incredibly proud.

Walker: I am! I tell him often, "You have made me proud. I couldn't be any prouder." And he has always supported his dad and me in our way of life.

Hughes: And then look what you've done in your community. You came here and you made a difference.

Walker: I keep remembering what it was like down South (in the 1940s). I remember when James came home one day and said, "Well, they want me to go..." someplace in the South. I can't remember if it was Georgia or Louisiana. But he said, "I hesitate to take you down South, honey." Because we had been down there visiting, you know, and then one day I went in the store to buy a pair of hose. I think I told you this story the other day.

Hughes: When you were in Louisiana.

Walker: In Louisiana. It was in 1943. And the sales clerk left me and went to wait on a white woman that came in. I went to the car and told James, "Get me out of this town. I'll kill somebody. I can't take this." The

A train trip in the 1960s: James Jr. and his mother sit behind his sister
June and their grandmother, Hazel Allen.

South was not for me.

Hughes: The South was not going to rise again on your watch!

Walker: Oooohhhh, no!

Hughes: If they'd were going to kill you for being black, you would
have taken somebody with you, wouldn't you?

Walker: Oh, I would have. Like I told you about the man at the restaurant, and he was going to come over to the counter and get me. And I
said, "You'll leave here without a part of you."

Hughes: It would be erroneous for me to compare you to Gandhi in
this profile, wouldn't it?! (laughing) You're all for non-violence, as a matter
of principle, but if somebody ...

Walker: You know, I hate to say I'm a fighter, but even as a kid, nobody
beat me. I'm not bragging.

Hughes: You've made a believer out of me, Mrs. Walker. You learned
early on to stand up for yourself.

Walker: I tried.

Hughes: But you're also a peace-loving person?

Walker: I try to be. I think you can work and negotiate and sit down and have a conference, and you get to speak your peace. I didn't say I was going to agree with you. I will discuss it with you. But there's that sign I've got in the bathroom? (laughing)

Hughes: It says, "You have the right to your opinion just as long as it agrees with mine."

Walker: And like I used to tell my kids, you know, you are the child and if God had meant you to be the ruler he would have figured out some other way that mothers didn't have to go through all that pain of having a baby. I don't know if it sunk in or not, but that's what I would tell them.

Hughes: My mother used to call me at 4:13 a.m. every year on October 22, my birthday. She'd wake me up and say, "This is your mother. I was in excruciating pain at this time in 1943. But I still love you and you're worth it."

Walker: (laughing) That's really cute!

Hughes: Tell me about the Ebenezer A.M.E. Church. Is it in the same place today as it was when you joined in October of 1941?

Walker: Yes, it is.

Hughes: If I go looking for the A.M.E. Church, where is it?

Walker: It's at 9th and Park. 902 Park Ave.

Hughes: A lot of people who hear the name think there is something goofy about "Methodist Episcopal." But "Episcopal" refers just to organizing; it's not the Anglican-style Episcopal Church.

Walker: It's a Methodist Church. The African Methodist Episcopal Church.

Hughes: Has that been a huge part of your life?

Walker: It has.

Hughes: What have you done in terms of church work? Have you had a key role as an elder over the years?

Walker: We went to Seattle one day. The missionary women of the church went to a meeting. And so they asked me, "Well, what office have you held in the church?" I said, "I've been everything but the minister." I was trustee. I was a steward. I was the secretary of the Sunday School. I've been on the trustees' board, and I've been on the steward board, and I've been the president of the Missionary Society. Like I told them, I've held every office in the Ebenezer A.M.E. Church except being the minister.

Hughes: They ought to ordain you down the stretch, just for drill.

Walker: No, no. I was once one of the minister's secretaries. So I'd go down there, and he drank. He had wine. I said, "Are you going to be drunk on Sunday mornings? I wonder what the congregation would say if they knew how much you drank." And this is a fact. "Don't you want a drink of wine?" he said. "No thank you. I'm working."

Hughes: Was he chastened by that? Did he get the message?

Walker: No. Well, I don't know.

Hughes: How long did that guy last?

Walker: Probably two years, maybe.

Hughes: And you've got a lady pastor now.

Walker: Oh Lord have mercy!

Hughes: You know, Judge Utter is a Baptist. He's the former state Supreme Court justice I interviewed earlier this year.

Walker: Is he?

Hughes: Yes. But he has more or less fallen out. You know, you and Judge Utter are a lot alike. He tries to be kind but he speaks his mind. I said, "Well, are you still real active in your church?" And he said, "Unfortunately, I'm not, because every Baptist congregation has the seeds of destruction sewn within each one—and that is the way they pick and change their pastors."

Walker: You know, in the back of the church in my home, back in Illinois they tell me that the preacher used to come there on a Sunday morning and he'd have the Bible here, and his pistol there. He'd say: "If you raise up against me, I'm going to shoot you."

Hughes: Are you kidding?

Walker: I guess you always had to agree with him. (laughing) You're not going to raise up!

Hughes: So, how many people are there in the congregation of the A.M.E. church? Is it bigger or smaller than it used to be?

Walker: It's smaller now, and it's getting smaller.

Hughes: How many people go there?

Walker: Oh, I'd say Sunday mornings there may be 30, 35.

Hughes: And back in the day?

Walker: Oh, we had the church full on a Sunday morning, you know.

Hughes: So, in your spare time while you were raising kids you also seem to be everywhere at once: You're showing the colors for equality; you're a founding member of the NAACP.

Walker: Yes, I'm one of them. I was at a program the other night to celebrate the 100th anniversary of the NAACP, and they had me stand up to be honored as a charter member (of the Bremerton chapter). They said they weren't going to give me another plaque because I already had a wall covered in plaques.

Hughes: And you're a founding member of the YWCA of Kitsap County.

Walker: Yeah, one of them.

Hughes: You're active in the Democratic Party.

Walker: Yes, I *was*.

Hughes: You were president of the Bremerton unit of Church Women United?

Walker: Yes.

Hughes: And you worked at the Black USO Club during World War II?

Walker: Yes.

Hughes: What did you do there?

Walker: Oh, just greeting people and being the go-between to make sure they were getting what they needed.

Robinson: It was at the Labor Temple on Burwell Street.

Hughes: And you were the recipient of the Golden Acorn award from the PTA?

Walker: Oh yeah.

Hughes: And you've been everything but a minister in the A.M.E. Church.

Walker: In the Ebenezer A.M.E. Church.

Hughes: We don't want to short-change Ebenezer.

Walker: Oh no.

Hughes: And you were former treasurer of the Bremerton Garden Club?

Walker: Yes, I used to belong.

Hughes: Did you help organize that?

Walker: No, they were going already. And one of my friends, she's passed now. She and I were good friends in PTA. She wanted me to join, and I joined. And I enjoyed it.

Hughes: In terms of gardening, you've got some amazing buttercups along the driveway. I don't know if they're wild or not, but they're gorgeous.

Walker: They're wild.

Hughes: (Addressing Robinson) I asked earlier about the black USO Club in Bremerton. Did they have black Shore Patrol as well as white Shore Patrol? Were they treating those black Navy sailors any different?

Robinson: I think they had some black Shore Patrol.

Walker: You know when the Negro soldiers couldn't do certain things, they got that broke up.

Hughes: What was the Carver Civic Club, Mrs. Walker?

Walker: It's a club that belongs to the National Association of Colored Women. And I guess I still am on the national board.

Hughes: Is that still active, the Carver Club?

Walker: *Oh yes.*

Hughes: What do those ladies do?

Walker: Dianne is a new member of it.

Robinson: Yeah, I got it going again. It is one of the oldest African-American organizations.

Walker: It is the oldest.

Robinson: Yeah, and they spread it out all over the United States, and they did that around 1896. They could help people in the community to build the moral conditions.

Walker: Yes. That's why they organized in 1896, because the white people thought that the Negro women were nothing but whores and prostitutes. And so they wanted to get that marked out and show people we are not women of the streets. We are upstanding. We are Christian. We believe in treating people right. And that was the philosophy behind their organization.

Robinson: It was also where they helped to educate. A lot of the school teachers were a part of those clubs. They were like a community connection to the people, as far as education goes.

Hughes: How have you done on diversifying faculties in Bremerton public schools? Are people of color pretty well represented now? I was shocked when I started doing work about Justice Smith to find out that so few judges in our state are people of color.

Robinson: That's the same thing here as far as the school district goes. You know, I really feel like they haven't made a great move either.

Walker: They haven't, no.

Robinson: I remember us recruiting the African-American teachers here back in the 1960s and I don't think they have hired many African-American teachers since then.

Walker: Except Alyce's daughter, Phyllis.

Hughes: Do you have any problem in recruiting African-Americans to Bremerton? What type of reputation does Bremerton have? If I would just stop somebody on the street who happened to be a person of color, what would they say about what kind of community Bremerton is in welcoming people of color?

Walker: I would think it depended on the person that you stopped, as to what they did. What would you say, Dianne?

Robinson: I would think that it probably would be very negative because we don't have a lot of representation on the boards. I'm the only (minority) city councilperson.

Walker: That's right. I don't think we've ever had another black City Council person.

Robinson: Yes we have. Al Colvin was on the council.

Walker: Oh yeah, Al.

Hughes: Was Al the first person of color in the history of the Bremerton City Council?

Robinson: Yes, I think Al was. And then there was Marty Crutcher. So there have been three.

EDITOR'S NOTE: Colvin died in 2008 at the age of 85. The civic pioneer was a member of the famed Tuskegee Airmen—the first group of Negro fighter pilots during World War II.

Al Colvin as a young Tuskegee Airman during World War II. *Black Historical Society of Kitsap County*

Walker: But if it was just an ordinary (minority) person that you just happened to see on the street, I don't think they would give you a positive answer.

Robinson: This area is still predominately white.

Hughes: Are you seeing a large influx of Hispanics folks?

Robinson: I've seen it here in the last two or three years. It's just amazing how many Hispanics are here now. That's a big change right there.

Walker: I know in this neighborhood we've seen it too.

Hughes: I want to be sure that I have my stories straight. In the Sinclair Park history project that Dianne worked on there's a little snippet of an oral history done with you, Mrs. Walker. And it's this story involving Chief Morken and Bill Simmons, another civil rights activist. Chief Morken was called to the scene after an incident involving Mr. Simmons at a "restaurant." Is that pretty much the same story you told earlier about your husband being refused service at the drug store?

Walker: No, that was at the Triangle Café down by the ferry terminal in the 1940s, where we had a "sit-in" in front of the establishment. We wouldn't leave until the chief of police got there. And we had a sit-in at another restaurant that was on 2nd Avenue. We always tried to get our point across without making another mess.

Hughes: So it was James and Bill Simmons (at the Triangle Café)?

Walker: Yes.

Hughes: But it sounds like *you* were there as well.

Walker: I was, and I think the minister was there, too. What was his name? How come I can't remember anything?

Hughes: Because you have too many things to remember.

Robinson: Cummings.

Walker: Yes, the Reverend Frank Cummings. He was the minister of our church at that time. And he met with Mr. Simmons and Chief Art Morken and the owner of the café.

Robinson: What year was that one?

Walker: It was around '43.

Robinson: Then that was E.P. Williams who was the minister. I have all that paperwork.

Walker: Oh, he was the minister who was involved?

Hughes: Well, here's what I've transcribed from that tape about the history of Sinclair Park. Chief Morken came along and said to Simmons, "What's going on here Bill?" And Bill said, "These people just don't want to serve us. They don't want to serve any Negroes. They just want to serve white people." So then the chief talked to them. Simmons and the chief met with the owner of the restaurant the next day.

Walker: On Monday. And he decided he would serve anybody that came in.

Hughes: The interviewer then turns to you, Mrs. Walker, and you say, "That was the start of ending some of the segregation in Bremerton, especially in eating places. Because if you can't treat your fellow man right and try to help better conditions for people that are coming behind you, well then why did you live?"

Walker: That sounds like me! (laughing)

Hughes: That's pretty much your credo isn't it?

Walker: That is right. That you're not here to mistreat people.

Hughes: That was pretty much what you always set out to do, wasn't it—create better conditions?

Walker: Oh yeah, you don't set up to tear somebody down. You are supposed to help people.

Hughes: I was interested to read that Quincy Jones Sr., a carpenter from Chicago, moved into Sinclair Heights in 1943, with his two sons, including Quincy Jr., who was very musical. Did you know young Quincy Jones?

Walker: I knew him but I didn't know him very personally, you know.

Hughes: So you didn't have any idea when you saw this bright boy that he was going to be one of the great musicians in American history?

Walker: No, I had no idea. Years later when I read about him, I said, "I knew that kid!"

Hughes: Did Quincy Jones come back to Bremerton over the years?

Walker: He has been here I think a couple of times after he got famous. But I never met him when he came. I would like to meet him. I'd say, "I knew you when you were a snotty nose."

Robinson: We've been trying to get him back here to do a project.

Hughes: That would be great.

Robinson: He had a show in Seattle, and when I went over to see if I could meet him I had found a picture, a 1943 picture, of him as a boy at Sinclair Park. And in the picture was a group of children. It was Easter Sunday, at the Sinclair Church, and there was Quincy Jones right in the middle of that. I met him and said, "Well, I have a picture of you." So he asked me to come up and bring the picture. He calls his brother from *behind* the stage. He said, "Come here—you won't believe this. This lady has got a picture of me in church when I was a kid." And he said, "I don't even remember being in church when I was a kid."

Hughes: That's wonderful. You've got this picture still?

Robinson: Yes.

Hughes: I'd like to see that. But you don't remember, Mrs. Walker, if you never upbraided Quincy or flattered him and told him he had a real talent?

Walker: If I did I don't remember. He didn't make a big impression.

Hughes: OK. Tell us about Sinclair Heights—about being postmaster up there, albeit for a short time. That was something important you achieved, after getting the top score on the test. You had a real opportunity there. And if it hadn't have been for you being devoted to being a mom, you might have gone someplace in the Post Office.

Walker: Oh I probably could have, yeah. Knowing me, I probably years later would have run for Carl Halverson's job. He was the Bremerton postmaster. At the time when he hired me, I joked, "Now, teach me all you know because I'm going to get your job."

Hughes: It's too bad you couldn't have stuck with that. With the chutzpah you have, you would have really gone places in the Post Office.

Walker: Mr. Halverson was very upset when I told him I was leaving. He hated to lose me. He was a real gentleman—a good white man. But my going places was lesser than being a mom. I wanted to raise my kids. I wanted to instill me in them, not somebody else teaching them what they wanted them to be. I just never could understand a woman that gives birth to a baby and then when it's a few months old she goes off to do her thing and somebody else is teaching her child. I didn't want that.

Hughes: What did you teach your children?

Walker: I tried to influence them to treat everybody like you like to be treated. You don't fight unless you have to. Things like that. And "tell the truth." My son and I went down here to the R & H Store one day. The R & H Market, a grocery store right down here on the highway. So we got home and he was writing with a pen. I said, "Where did you get that pen?" "I got it down at the store." "Did you buy it?" "No." "OK, you're going to take it back and tell them that you stole." And it never happened again.

Hughes: How old was Jimmy at that time?

Walker: He was probably 5 or 6, maybe 7. *He knew better.* I said, "You don't steal. Why didn't you buy the pen, or ask me to buy it for you?" He didn't think about it, he just saw the pen and he wanted it. I said, *"We don't do that."*

Hughes: Tell me about your grandchildren?

Walker: June has three—a boy and two girls. And Jimmy has two girls and a boy. The youngest one is going to Syracuse University and she graduates next year. Jimmy called me yesterday. "Mom can I put you down for a hotel room for..." and gave me the date of her graduation. I said, "I don't know whether I'll be alive." "Well, if you're alive." So he gave me the dates and I called June, because I can't come by myself. I wouldn't dare.

Hughes: So, do you get to see your grandkids? Are they all over?

Walker: I see them once in a while. Sometimes when Jimmy comes home for the summer Ashley will come back, too. Allison, the oldest one, has moved to New York. Her first job she worked in Kentucky. So one day she said, "Grandma, I don't like my boss." I said, "Why don't you study and get a new job?" "I don't want a new job." And I said, "Then quit complaining about her. Just be so nice to her—nice enough to kill her."

Hughes: I asked you about Barack Obama yesterday and I'd like you to think about it again because it's such a defining moment in American history. Did you work hard for Obama?

Walker: No, not hard because I had broken my hip. But every time I had a chance, I would. Like one day a man called me. He was taking a political poll. He was asking me different questions and then he got around to, "Are you a Democrat or a Republican?" I said, "I told you in the beginning, I'm a Democrat. I'm for Obama." "Oh, that's right you did." I said, "Well, don't forget it because I have never been a Republican, and I will never be a Republican. And I will support him because I think he's the best thing that has entered on the scene in politics. He's the man. We need him."

Hughes: And it's really not so much an issue of color, is it?

Walker: No. It's no color. He *knows* what he's doing. When he's giving a speech he has done all the research he can. Like, I saw him one day on TV talking to the press, and he said, "I haven't read it yet, and I can't give you an answer about a report until I read it."

Hughes: Did you like that line when they were talking about how he had promised the kids a dog? And he said, "We are looking for a shelter dog—a mutt like me."

Walker: Ooohhh, I didn't hear that! (laughing) But one day somebody asked them, "How is the dog coming along?" And Michelle says, "Oh, he tore up a book last night."

Hughes: She's a remarkable woman too.

Walker: She *sure* is. She sure is. I'm telling you.

Hughes: And those darling little girls, my gosh; they make a nice first family.

Walker: You know they took them to Europe with them?

Hughes: Paris. What a neat opportunity for those kids.

Walker: I thought that was really nice.

Hughes: So, you were sitting here watching your old RCA TV on election night. What were you thinking?

Walker: That I wouldn't be in that crowd up there (in Chicago) for nothing.

Hughes: Yeah, Oprah Winfrey was there and Jesse Jackson was there.

Robinson: I was there too!

Walker: Yeah, she was there.

Hughes: That must have been electric. So, Mrs. Walker, from your birth in 1913 to this amazing year of 2008, did you ever think you'd live to see a person of color being elected President of the United States?

Walker: No. I hoped, but I never thought it would happen in my lifetime. But the first time I heard Obama speak, I said, "That's the man. He can do it."

Hughes: I thought it might be General Powell.

Walker: Obama surpasses Powell by a mile. He's way ahead of Powell, *I* think.

Hughes: And how about some of your other heroes, regardless of color, in your lifetime. Who have you really admired?

Walker: I admired Franklin Roosevelt. And I met him when he came to Bremerton.

Hughes: Tell me about that!

Walker: Well, it was just, "I'm Mrs. Walker, Mr. President. Glad to meet you." You know, stuff like that.

Hughes: Was he classically FDR—gracious?

Walker: Oh he was very gracious, yes.

Hughes: Wonderful smile?

Walker: Yes!

Hughes: Was he riding in a car?

Walker: No, he was in a wheelchair.

Hughes: You saw FDR in a wheelchair? Isn't that interesting?

Walker: It's really interesting.

Hughes: But you're sure he was in a wheelchair?

Walker: I'm sure, yeah.

Hughes: I ask that because he wore steel braces on his legs because he'd had polio, and there was a subterfuge by his staff, with the assistance of the press, to create the impression that he wasn't so crippled, to make him look more robust. But late in the war when he was really fatigued, they sometimes were less guarded.

Walker: Well, he was *sitting*. He was not standing. I never shook his hand when he was standing.

Hughes: And what was the occasion?

Walker: The Democrats were having something here. I don't remember.

Robinson: He went to the Ship Yard. Actually, he came here twice, in 1942 and 1944.

Hughes: Mrs. Walker must have met him the second time. His son-in-law and daughter came out here to manage the *Seattle P-I*—John and Anna Boettiger.

Robinson: Yes.

Walker: It *was* in 1944.

Hughes: What did he say to you? What were his words, Mrs. Walker?

Walker: Oh, "Glad to meet you," or something. I was just a nobody.

Hughes: But did you shake his hand?

Walker: Oh yeah.

Hughes: And did he look you in the eye?

Walker: Oh yeah.

EDITOR'S NOTE: Roosevelt's visit to the Navy Yard in 1942 was one of the best kept secrets of the war, even though he spoke to yard workers. They were admonished not to talk about it. FDR visited the Navy Yard again on August 12, 1944, at which time he made a nationwide radio broadcast from the prow of a destroyer.

Hughes: Who are some of your other political heroes?

Walker: Oh Lord, that's a tough question.

Hughes: Are there some state representatives that you've worked hard for over the years who have done a good job for Kitsap County?

Walker: Yeah, and Governor Rosellini—we went to his ball at the Capitol.

Hughes: You went to the Inaugural Ball for Governor Rosellini?

Walker: Well, had a party at the Capitol and we were there. Adele (Ferguson) was there.

Hughes: This is a good story already. I can feel it coming on.

Walker: They had food, and they had chitlins.

Hughes: Chitlins?

Walker: Chitlins. And they had different kinds of food on the table. We had all gone around and gotten a plate, you know. And Adele said, "I love those things. What are they?" And I said, "Those are Kentucky Oysters."

Hughes: "Kentucky oysters"? What is that?

Walker: That's what the old-fashioned name for them is. Chitlins. You don't say those are "hog guts," you know. I said, "Help yourself, lady! They don't care. They've got whatever you can eat." Adele loved those things. She was bragging on them.

Hughes: Who brought the chitlins?

Walker: I have no idea. I'll have to ask Adele the next time I see her, "You remember the Kentucky Oysters?" (laughing)

Hughes: That is so funny. Have any other governors been here who have been particularly good for Kitsap County?

Walker: I don't really know. But one of the things about the 23rd District is they enlarged it. And then they called me, and wanted me to run again for precinct committee officer. And I said, "No, because you increased my precinct and I cannot cover it. And I don't want something that I can't do my job in."

Hughes: You were precinct committeewoman for the 23rd District?

Walker: Yes. Oh, I did that for I don't know how many years.

Hughes: Did you go to any of those national conventions over the years?

Walker: No, I never went to any.

Hughes: How about the state ones?

Walker: I went to some state conventions. Like one time there was something in Yakima where James and I took the bus over there. But, I never went to a national, no.

Hughes: So, when did James retire from the job there in Seattle? Was he taking the ferry across every day?

Walker: Yeah, he was taking the ferry or driving his car, most of the time, though, he'd take his car and park it in the parking lot. That's when we came to have two cars because he bought a Toyota to ride the ferry.

Hughes: So when was it that he retired?

Walker: He worked 39 years and if he could have worked one more year then he would have had 40 years in the service. And he started in '41, so it was '79. I believe that was the year he retired. And I said, "Well, if you work six more months..." He came home one day and he said, "I think I'm trying to have another heart attack!"

Hughes: Had he had a heart attack?

Walker: He had had a heart attack, yes. And so, when he came home that night, we were working at the bank doing janitorial work, and he came home and he was hurting. He wanted a couple of aspirins.

Hughes: Did that help?

Walker: Oh yeah. But, Monday morning I called the doctor and told him the problem. He said, "I think you ought to bring James in." He had had a heart attack. So, the doctor sent him to Seattle, to Swedish Hospital. The doctor, he's an elderly man. And when we got through, he set him up with an appointment to come back for an operation. So, we came home and I called his local doctor and I took James in and I told him what the Seattle doctor said. I said, "He wants to operate on him." He said, "I didn't send you to Seattle for medical advice. I sent you to see if he agreed with me that he had had a heart attack. But he didn't have any heart damage." So when the (Seattle) doctor called James, James said, "I won't be there." The doctor said, "Let me talk to Mrs. Walker." And I said, "Well, I took him to his doctor and his doctor said he didn't send him over there to see you to make an appointment for an operation. He just wanted you to agree or disagree on whether he had a heart attack."

Hughes: A second opinion.

Walker: A second opinion, exactly. And I said, "No, we won't be there. The doctor said he doesn't have any heart damage, and he does not need any surgery." But see, we had Blue Shield, our insurance. So his local doctor said, "He's looking at the money. He wasn't looking at his health, (just) how much money he could get out of this one operation."

Hughes: Please tell me this has a happy ending. So did James do well after that?

Walker: He did. Dr. Harris, his doctor here said, "He doesn't have any heart damage."

Hughes: So please tell me that you and James got to have a happy retirement together before he passed away.

Walker: We always had things together.

Hughes: What did you do?

Walker: Well, sometimes we'd decide to go to restaurants that we didn't ordinarily go to, or things like that. We always had a nice time.

Hughes: And when did James leave us?

Walker: He died in 2000.

Hughes: How old was James?

Walker: Let's see, he was born in 1911. He was 89.

Hughes: So, you married an "older guy"?

Walker: Well, he was only two years older.

Hughes: I'm kidding you!

Walker: If I had searched the world over I couldn't have found a better mate. He was a good husband. He was a good father. He was a good son. Well, I think he was a good son. (laughing) One day I said, "Did you call your mother this week?" "No." So he got on the phone and called his mother. "Well, Lillian told me that I should call you." His mother said, "Why does Lillian have to tell you to call me?"

Hughes: James was a lucky man. My mom always said that the best thing about people who were so alive when they were alive is that when they're gone, they've never really gone. You expect them to walk in the room.

Walker: Oh Lord, tell me about!

Hughes: I can tell from that guy's smile in that photo. Boy, he's a good-looking man.

Walker: *Oh Lord*, the other night I looked over (at his picture) and I could see him coming through the door. Or, I go to bed... "OK, honey, I got the bed warmed for you!" And he says, "OK, put your cold foot up on my leg." That's what I heard for 40 years. Now I've got to put on socks.

Hughes: That's wonderful!...Back to less happy stuff one last time: You were quoted, just last year, as saying that when you came to Bremerton it was "a white supremacist town."

James and Lillian Walker in their retirement years.

Walker: Well, it was.

Hughes: And so all these years later, has it changed?

Walker: Oh yeah, yeah, I think so. There has been a lot of change, I think.

Hughes: It helps to have a councilwoman like that, doesn't it? (pointing to Robinson)

Walker: Oh Heaven's, I just hate to see her retire. Jeeze, she's been great.

Hughes: You're not going to retire, are you? Are you running for election?

Robinson: No, I'm not up. I've got two more years. I wish I had the finances to do what I really want to do because, you know, there is so much rich history here.

Walker: In that field, you're doing great.

Robinson: I've worked so hard doing research. I've spent hours and hours pulling this stuff together. And once you pull it together, you know, it's fascinating. I just thank God because I believe this is the gift God has given me—this community. Because there was not a whole lot of information. There were only a few words (about black history) here and there in the history books that they have written about Kitsap County. But even before Bremerton became Bremerton, the first man here, the first white man, said that there was a black man here with an Indian wife and 10 children. That was John Garrison. And if you go and research John Garrison in history you'll see how much land that he cultivated in the area.

Walker: Was he the man you told about that they wanted to go to Oregon, and he wouldn't do it because Oregon was so prejudiced?

Robinson: Yes. Oregon forbid its blacks. They couldn't live there. But Mrs. Walker is talking about Nathaniel Sargent, who was elected the Justice of Peace in Seabeck, Washington, in 1894. He owned just acres and acres out there. I have all his written diaries....(History) has a place in my heart. I feel so good when I put the bits and pieces together. And now I'm working with her church...the whole history of the A.M.E. Church, from the Civil War to the present.

Walker: Oh really? Bless your heart.

Robinson: I went to North Carolina and found ministers that actually were preachers here in this area at her church. I found at least 80 ministers' pictures. And I can put the ministers with the time they were here.

Hughes: (to Mrs. Walker) You lived through the Great Depression but one of the ironies is that when you were in the Depression your folks were so poor that you hardly even knew it.

Walker: We had plenty of food, you know. The worst I remember in the food line was one Sunday morning we didn't have cornbread for breakfast because dad forgot to get flour on Saturday in town. Now we thought that was *terrible* because we were used to biscuits for breakfast.

Hughes: Being the only girl there, did you help your mom with a lot of the cooking?

Walker: I don't know if I told you this yesterday or not. Mom couldn't read.

Hughes: Yes. You told me that.

Walker: And I would read, so I read to her while she was cooking, whatever she wanted to hear—magazines, newspapers, books…

Hughes: Because mom was not any way a "dumb" person, was she?

Walker: Oh no, oh no, no. She would gather her eggs from the hen and whoever took the eggs to town she knew how much they were a dozen, and how much money she had coming back. She skimmed the cream off of milk and they had a little place in town, in Carrier Mills, and she could sell that cream. She knew how much cream she had, she could count money. She didn't have any trouble counting money.

Hughes: Did your mother live long enough to see her grandson Jimmy do really well, get his Ph.D.? When did your mom die?

Walker: Let's see, it was the late '60s.

Hughes: Oh, okay, so Jimmy was in school and was doing well. Was she proud of him?

Walker: *Oh Heavens*, she was proud of her grandkids. Yes she was.

Hughes: How about dad? How old did he live to be?

Walker: He died in '66.

Hughes: And the two of them came out and lived out here?

Walker: Yes.

Hughes: Were they just surviving pretty much on their Social Security?

Walker: You know, I wouldn't meddle into their affairs, but if they needed something, we helped. We always picked them up and took them to church, or wherever they wanted to go, shopping or whatever. And dad spent a lot of time at the bus stop right out from their house. He'd go out there. He loved to talk to people. You want to know where I got my talkativeness? (laughing) And he'd sit out there, talking with people waiting on the bus. And they'd say, "Well, Moses you going to go?" "No, I'm just sitting here visiting." And he'd sit there and visit with people half a day or so.

Hughes: When you look at this recession that's hitting people so hard, are there any kind of lessons you learned during the Depression that you wished people really understood better?

Walker: You know, I was not at that point taking part in the family affairs or anything. And I don't remember Mom and Dad discussing finances. But I remember one time, Mom and us kids were going to town to visit Aunt Cassie. And Aunt Cassie was being nosy about mom, whether she has money, and she came home telling dad and he said, "Did you tell her that you had $150 in your pocket?" She said, "No, I didn't think she needed to know that." So, they got along. And when James and I were living in '42 in an apartment down on Dick Turpin's apartment house, and we were signed up to a bank and so the bank statement came. And at the end of the month I said, "OK, we're going to balance the bank book." We were off a penny. My husband said, "Well, here's a penny." I said, "We don't balance a checkbook like that!" But as I said before, James was a good husband and a good father.

Hughes: And when he retired, what was his job at that time? He was in electronics, is that right?

Walker: He was in electronics, electricity; he did the electricity on three ships. He was the electrical person. And so he came home one day and he was going to retire. Someone made him angry on one of the ships. I said, "*Wait a minute.* You don't just up and retire like that. You give me six months and I'll have all the credit cards paid off and everything in order. Then you can retire, and we can live off your retirement. "OK honey." And he did that. And so when I got every card paid off, everything, no bills at all, I said, "OK, go to it. Go tell them take this job and shove it!" (laughing)

Hughes: Any regrets? Anything that you'd like to do over?

Walker: I don't know how I would have done it over. I always would have liked to go to school. But I liked being a housewife, and I liked being a mother and I didn't envision anything that was going to take me from that.

Hughes: You would have been a great doctor. That was always in the back of your head wasn't it?

Walker: I liked that. I liked working with patients. And people that came into the office. The doctor had an array of white and black, different races of people. That was in Harrisburg, Illinois.

Hughes: Just down the road from...

Walker: Carrier Mills, yes.

Hughes: If you go online now and you plug in Carrier Mills is there still a place there?

Walker: Still there.

Hughes: Any kinfolk still there that you know of?

Walker: Oh yeah, my oldest brother, his kids. Well, I have two nieces and a nephew that live in that area. And they have been most congenial calling me to see how Aunt Lillian is. At least every month Lewis calls. He's named after my brother, and he lives in Centralia, which is, say, 40 miles from Carrier Mills.

Hughes: Central Illinois.

Walker: Right. He and his wife and family live there. He has a daughter or a granddaughter in California. And most of the time he'd call me from there, to check on me, to see how I am. And he would come and visit us once in a while. Especially Ulysses, and we'd all go over there.

Hughes: I love the name Ulysses; that's just a great name.

Walker: Yeah, I don't know how mom and dad came up with it: Ulysses Grant Allen.

Hughes: It probably was from U.S. Grant....So, I guess the all-time classic question is this: How do you figure you got to live to be almost 100 years old, and with your faculties intact?

Walker: I don't miss a day, or a night, telling God thank you for not taking my brain because someone asked me the other day, "How do you compare 95 to…" I said, "I've never known anybody 95, so I don't know what I've got to compare it to."

Hughes: I've known quite a few people who have been 95, and you're the first one I've ever met who is as sharp as you are.

Walker: Well, whatever I go into, I go into with confidence. It's just like when I read Adele's transcript here, her history, when she got to be a reporter without going to journalism school. She said, "Well I know most of that. I can do this!"

Hughes: I hope you will read Charles Z. Smith's oral history, too.

Walker: That's what I want to do.

Hughes: If he were in Bremerton, you and C.Z. Smith would be dear friends. The only thing different, actually, between Charles Z. Smith and Lillian Walker is that when he was a young boy he was befriended by a college president.

Walker: Oh really?

Hughes: He spotted Charles as being a bright boy, and he became his mentor. And he paid his way through college.

Walker: Oh isn't that something!

Hughes: If Lillian Allen would have had something like that…

Walker: Oh, wouldn't that have been wonderful!? But then I've had a good life. After I met James and I just knew that he was the one.

Hughes: Had you had serious boyfriends before James?

Walker: Oh, I've had a couple. And one of them, I think I told you yesterday, the man had slapped me.

Hughes: Yeah, and that was the end of him.

Walker: Right. But I know when my girlfriend introduced me to James, there was something special. His ideas and mine were the same. And when he came to Washington, I wrote him a letter to tell him what I'd been do-ing, especially cooking. He said, "You make me hungry."

Hughes: You're a good cook, aren't you?

Walker: Well, I try to be. And you know my mother taught my brother how to cook. Both of my brothers could cook, Lewis and Ulysses. Because

Ulysses used to say, "You know what I had for dinner last night, sis?" And I'd say, "No." "I had a steak and salad." I said, "What did Naomi say?" "She wanted me to have some potatoes, and I told her I didn't want her potatoes. I just wanted steak and salad." And my son Jimmy can cook. When they first started keeping house he'd call me and say, "Mom, mom, how do you make pie crust?" He'd go to the store and buy pie crust. I said, "Well, you take some flour and shortening." By the way, we had a Filipino family that lived across the street and they had three girls.

Hughes: Has this always been an integrated neighborhood?

Walker: Yes. Well, we were the first off-race people that moved in to any part of here. And I think there was a black family that lives up on up the street, but I'm not sure.

Hughes: And no problem from the beginning?

Walker: No, the only one that we had—well it wasn't trouble. It was like the little white boys that would say things—little boys who were 3 and 4 years old.

Hughes: They didn't know any better.

Walker: No, they had been taught that. But one of the girls on the block, I'd usually bake them a pie or something for their birthday. So one of them said, "Grandma Walker—" Well, they first asked could they call me grandma. I said, "Sure." So she said, "Can you teach me how to make that pie? I want to know from the crust on up." I said, "The day you want it, you come over, and when I put the flour in the bowl, you take it out and make it. Because I don't make it from a recipe."

Hughes: You know it by heart.

Walker: I know what I do, and how much it takes. "Then when I put the salt in I'll let you measure it before I put it in." So the first one she made she called me and told me, "I made the pie." "How did it do?" "It's good." I said, "OK, you're on your way." But Jimmy still calls me once in a while about cooking. And one time he said, "Well, I'm the best spaghetti cook in Cincinnati." I said, "You've got your daddy beat. Your daddy couldn't boil water."

Hughes: Do you have any favorite Bible verses that are really close to your heart?

Walker: You know they were doing that the Sunday before last at church. And people were getting up saying, "Such and such." So I got up and said, "Well, I don't have a perfect Bible verse. It depends on the occasion. And one of my favorite things is doing unto others as I would have them do unto me."

Hughes: It doesn't get any better than that does it?

Walker: Well, I don't think so.

Hughes: Any words of wisdom to live by? Advice for people who read this about how to be a happy person and to appreciate life?

Walker: Don't complain. If you've got something to complain about, well, work at it and make it better. That's what I told my granddaughter when she was complaining about her boss. "OK, go to school and study and you can get her job." "I don't want her job." I said, "Well, then, stop complaining." And, treat everybody right. I don't care what, who, what they are, treat them right. You don't have the authority to mistreat anybody, because that's why we are here, to help each other. If you can help somebody, help them.

Hughes: Racism has to be the most evil conceit there is.

Walker: Oh my Lord!

Hughes: I mean to think of all the horrible things that have been done on account of prejudice.

Walker: I just can't imagine people being as evil as some of them are.

Hughes: Do you remember that wonderful musical, *South Pacific*? Nellie, the Navy nurse, is from Little Rock, Arkansas, and she still harbors prejudice in her heart. And they sing a song, "You have to be carefully taught." That you weren't born to hate, that people have to be taught to hate.

Walker: That's where the problem starts—teaching your family how to hate. And I tried *never* to mistreat any kid. I tried to teach my kids that you don't mistreat anybody. And you respect *all* your elders, whether they're kin or not. If Cousin Jamie is going to be over there, you call her Aunt Jamie, and you respected her. I can't remember ever in my life calling an elderly person by their first name. You know, sometimes now, I pray, I ask God, "What are you keeping me here for?" And God says, "You're doing it." I say, "Well, what am I doing?" "Well, you're nice to everybody." But I tell Him, "I've always been nice to people."

Hughes: You believe the Lord has spoken to you over the years, hasn't he? You've really heard it, haven't you?

Walker: Right.

Hughes: That tells me that there's a powerful force in your life, and always has been.

Walker: Thank the Lord.

Hughes: With all the sweat equity you've invested in making Bremerton a better place—to "straighten out this town," as you put it, do you worry about the younger generation getting complacent now that so many civil rights victories have been won?

Walker: Oh definitely!

Hughes: What advice do you have for these young people?

Walker: Well, one time (in recent years) I was over at the school and the young people, they were acting up; they were noisy; they had their caps on their heads. And I told them, "If I was your teacher, you wouldn't come to school like that!" And someone said, "How come you didn't become a teacher?" and I said, "Because I'd kill one of you kids! (chuckling). Well, I wouldn't kill him, but I'd make him think he was dying."

Hughes: But what advice do you have for these young people who take for granted these freedoms that you fought for?

Walker: I'd try to tell them, "You don't know what you're doing.... Know your history! We have fought for you to have the rights to go in and sit down and eat, to go and apply for a job." And I'd tell them you don't go around with your pants hanging down your behind like you can almost see the crack of your behind! You don't do that and get ahead." One day Jimmy came home and said, "Mom, you know the boys at school they go around with their shirt tail out?" And I said, "If I come to school and your shirt tail is out I'm going to show you where it belongs!"

Hughes: So your advice to these young black people is that you'd better be more vigilant?

Walker: Or it's going to go downhill. And you've got kids killing one another over drugs and gangs.

Hughes: Is there a question that you wish I had asked that you wanted to answer? A story that didn't come up that you really wanted to tell me that's really important to your life?

Walker: If they come to my mind I'll try to do that.

Hughes: You are one of the most amazing people I've ever met. Thank you so much for taking this time.

Walker: Well, thank you. You've been great.

Hughes: Well, the feeling's likewise.

Walker: I'm going to keep calling you "Judge Hughes" if you don't mind.

Hughes: I've always wanted to be a judge! And I will call you "Doctor Walker" because you should have been a doctor.

Walker: (Laughing) OK!

EDITOR'S NOTE: Judge Robin Hunt of the Washington Court of Appeals introduced Hughes to Mrs. Walker, and she thought he was a judge, too.

END OF INTERVIEW

Secretary of State Sam Reed, left, and John C. Hughes with Lillian Walker in 2009 when her oral history was first published. Reed established The Legacy Project in 2008. Hughes joined the Office of the Secretary of State as chief oral historian in 2008 after a 42-year career in journalism.

ACKNOWLEDGMENTS & FOOTNOTES

It was Judge Robin Hunt of the Washington Court of Appeals who first told The Legacy Project about Lillian Walker and her inspirational life. Secretary of State Sam Reed and my Legacy Project teammates, Trova Heffernan and Lori Larson, also became charter members of the Lillian Walker Admiration Society, together with former secretary of state Ralph Munro. Thanks also to the following for their assistance in telling her story: Dianne Robinson and the Black Historical Society of Kitsap County; Dr. James T. Walker Jr.; Carolyn Neal and the Kitsap Regional Library; Linda Joyce of the YWCA of Kitsap County; Charles Horton and Jim Campbell of *The Kitsap Sun;* Professor Quintard Taylor, founder of BlackPast.org; Charles Z. Smith, retired justice of the Washington State Supreme Court; Don Brazier, Washington State legislative historian; Andy Oakley and the Bremerton Police Department; Bonnie Chrey and the Kitsap County Historical Society Museum; Danelle Feddes, Heather Mygatt and the Puget Sound Navy Museum; Cristy Gallardo and the Puget Sound Naval Shipyard; David Nicandri, director of the Washington State Historical Society; Adele Ferguson, Bremerton's famous columnist, and Lillian's dear friends, Alyce Eagans, Hazel and Althea Colvin.

While interviewing Mrs. Walker, I was struck by a passage from Ronald C. White Jr.'s critically acclaimed biography, "A. Lincoln." Heartsick as the Know-Nothings made inroads into the Whig Party, Lincoln wrote to his old friend Joshua Speed in 1854: "Our progress in degeneracy appears to me to be pretty rapid. As a nation, we began by declaring that 'all men are created equal.' We now practically read it, 'all men are created equal, except negroes.' When the Know-Nothings get control, it will read 'all men are created equal, except negroes, and foreigners, and catholics.' When it comes to this, I should prefer emigrating to some country where they make no pretence of loving liberty—Russia, for instance, where despotism can be taken pure, without the base alloy of hypocrisy."

—*John Hughes*, 2010

A famous son of Sinclair Heights: For a comprehensive history of the Bremerton Shipyard, see *NIPSIC to Nimitz by* Louise M. Reh and Helen Lou Ross (ISBN 0-931475-02-3, Naval Memorial Museum of the Pacific, Bremerton, 1991.) It takes note of a Sinclair Heights boy destined for greatness in the music world: "Quincy Jones Sr., a carpenter from Chicago, and his two sons arrived at Sinclair Heights on July 4, 1943. Their house was small and poorly heated, but for the boys it was a wonderful place; it was in a wooded area with much to explore and wild berries to eat. The older boy had been interested in music while in Chicago; now he received encouragement from musicians in the Navy Yard and from teachers in Bremerton Schools," including Joseph Powe, who had a dance band on the side. A barber named Eddie Lewis also gave him some pointers, Jones recalls.

In *The Complete Quincy Jones*, an autobiography (Insight Editions, San Rafael, CA, 2008, ISBN: 13:978-1-933784-67-0), Jones documents the discrimination his father faced in trying to keep a job in the industrial wing of the national defense program in Chicago, despite the fact that he was an expert carpenter. One day, when he picked up his sons after work, he abruptly announced, "We're leaving." Quincy Jr., who was 10, sputtered, "Can we get our toys?" Daddy said no. "We don't have time." They hopped a Trailways bus and headed for Bremerton. "They had a place way out of town called Sinclair Heights," Jones says. "We had to walk up a hill forever, three miles. That's where they put all the black people."

Paul de Barros, an author and music critic, features Jones in his book on the roots of jazz in Seattle, *Jackson Street After Hours* (ISBN 0-912365-86-2,

Sasquatch Books, Seattle, 1993). In it, Jones recalls that the government and the white power structure in Bremerton made sure that Sinclair Heights "was way away from town....They also didn't put phones in the homes. You had to go to a telephone booth. They didn't want the black people to get so comfortable there after the war. They wanted them to get out."

In a vignette entitled "Delin-Quincy" in his own book, Quincy recalls, "When I got to Bremerton, an armory was our recreation center. We heard there was a new shipment of ice cream coming in with some lemon meringue pie. We thought that this was a great chance for us to use all of our training with the greatest gangsters in the world as kids. So we broke in there, ate up the pie, and roamed around..." He ended up in the supervisor's office, and had a life-changing encounter with "a little spinet piano over in the corner." He "touched it, and every cell in my body and every drop of blood said, 'This is what you're gonna do the rest of your life.' So I stayed and practiced the piano all day after that." The rest, as they say, is history.

When they moved to Seattle in 1947, Jones attended Garfield, Seattle's most diverse high school. On trumpet, he was a star performer with the school band and hailed as a prodigy by the local dailies. With his own band and other combos, he often had three gigs a night, and his arrangements were played by the likes of Count Basie. He also met an amazingly eclectic teenage musician from Florida who had been blind since childhood, Ray Charles Robinson. Ray was playing at the Black Elks Club on the north side of Seattle's Jackson Street. "Q" and Ray Charles became legends in their own time. Jones has won 27 Grammys, including one for producing "Thriller," Michael Jackson's landmark pop fusion album. He is also an internationally honored humanitarian who produced "We are the world."

Lillian Walker remembers encountering Quincy Sr. when she managed the Sinclair Heights Post Office, but neither of his livewire sons made a big impression. "Years later when I read about Quincy, I'd say, 'I knew that kid!' But I really didn't know him....He sure is a brilliant man!"

De Barros' book, which features a photo gallery by Eduardo Calderon, also notes the racial culture tension in Seattle as a throng of southern

Negroes arrived to work in the war industry: "For a while, there was friction between the older black community and the new arrivals." The newcomers wore dungarees on the street, tied their heads in handkerchiefs, ate watermelon on the curb and were "noisy." And "though no one dared speak publicly of it, there was also an issue of skin tone within the black community. The new immigrants, largely from the Southwest and the South, were not only more rural, less educated and 'ill-mannered,' they were also darker-skinned."

The "Negro Problem": Nard Jones' widely read 1947 book *Evergreen Land, A Portrait of the State of Washington,*" commented on black and Hispanic migration to Washington in the 1940s. Jones wrote that in World War II, "With the Army and the Navy and the Coast Guard naturally came the workers. Towns that had rarely glimpsed a Negro accustomed themselves (or did not) to Negroes by the hundreds. Some of the Negroes were from the deep South and not too happy in the far Northwest, but they were happier than the Mexicans who were brought in by rail and truck to act as farm labor. To a Mexican the Pacific Northwest is a dismal place indeed, where the sun shines briefly or not at all. They did not sing very much, those Mexicans....They have departed from the Evergreen Land now and are glad of it. But the Negroes, most of them, have wanted to stay."

Earlier, Jones focused on what he saw as the genesis of "the Negro problem" in Washington, noting that Captain William Clark of the famed Lewis and Clark Expedition (1804-06) brought along a Negro—"a six-footer called York." "The fact that he was the slave of Captain Clark, and black, does not seem to have depressed him. He liked to jig for the awed savages by the camp fire and he delighted in performing feats of strength for them. Our western romanticists to the contrary, he was probably of more value to the safety of the party, therefore, than Sacajawea. Until World War II, Oregon and Washington were unfamiliar with the Negro problem. Now that they know what a Negro is, it is of historic interest to note that York, a bona fide member of the party of Lewis and Clark, was undoubtedly the first colored emigrant to the Pacific Northwest."

Lewis and Clark scholar David Nicandri, the director of the Washington State Historical Society, sets the record straight in several instances: He is aware of no known basis for asserting York's stature. As for the notion that York was not depressed to be a slave, "not during the time of the expedition perhaps, but our impression for that fact would have been Clark's own journal; hardly an objective source on the matter. It is known, after the expedition, that York took considerable objection to his status and Clark's unwillingness to free him." Moreover, "rarely was the party's 'safety' in jeopardy, and probably the one time it was, on the Bad River confluence with the Missouri, the flatboat's swivel gun was the dispositive element." Concerning Sacajawea's value to the expedition, "here Jones seems to be anticipating an argument that became popular much later, that she was some sort of an ambassador for the party." Jones' assertion that until World War II, Oregon and Washington were unfamiliar with "the Negro problem" is "an exaggeration to be sure," Nicandri adds. "There were slaves here, illicitly, in the 1850's. Settlers out this way were quite aware of the slavery issue." Characterizing York as the first colored emigrant to the Pacific Northwest, "depends on your definition of 'colored,'" the respected historian says. "If we mean 'people of color' in contemporary usage, definitely not. I like to tell people that if we saw the first non-Indian settlers of Washington today we would recognize them as being of Mexican ancestry. Neah Bay, 1790."

A medal long overdue? Dianne Robinson, founder and curator of the Black Historical Society of Kitsap County, has documented the arrival of blacks and Filipinos at the Puget Sound Navy Yard. Her research indicates there were more than 200 blacks in the Sinclair Inlet area by 1912 and most of the men worked at the Navy Yard. One was the legendary John Henry "Dick" Turpin (1876-1962), a U.S. Navy chief gunner's mate who retired in Bremerton in the 1920s and went to work as a master rigger driver at the Navy Yard. He was also a master diver. His wife Fay was a rivet passer during World War I. "Tall, erect and courtly," Turpin had been one of the Navy's first African American chief petty officers. He was highly respected in the Bremerton area, providing lodging to newly arriving blacks, including James and Lillian Walker. Handsome as a movie star, even in his 70s he could do handstands. Robinson and other black historians believe Turpin should have received the Medal of Honor, for which he was reportedly nominated not once but twice during his Navy service. A strong swimmer, he survived the sensational explosion that decimated the battleship *U.S.S. Maine* in Havana Harbor in 1898, and is credited with heroic life-saving efforts in the wake of the blast. In 1905, Turpin was aboard *the U.S.S. Bennington* in San Diego Harbor when its boiler exploded, and he saved the lives of several shipmates. He is also credited with helping invent the underwater cutting torch. During World War II, Turpin made "inspirational visits" to Naval Training Centers and defense plants, and was a guest of honor on the reviewing stand in Seattle when the first black volunteers were sworn into the Navy shortly after the attack on Pearl Harbor. See this link: **www.spanamwar.com/Turpin.html** Meantime, some 200 Native Americans worked in the Navy Yard during World War II, including Daniel Working Bull, the grandson of Sitting Bull.

A revered cop: Arthur Norman "Art" Morken (1909-1986), the Bremerton police chief fondly remembered by civil rights activists, joined the force in 1934 and quickly rose through the ranks to captain in 1941. He was acting chief during the tumultuous war years and became chief in 1961 with the retirement of Charles "Slats" Lewis. After retiring the following year, Morken was elected Kitsap County sheriff and served until retiring again in 1979. As a youth, Morken was a lifeguard at Lions Beach on Kitsap Lake and "saved many lives." Part of Morken's legacy, according to the Police Department's Web site, "was his love of children. He is remembered for starting the Safety Patrol Program and taught kids life-long values that he shared and instructed in the program. He instilled values such as respect for elders, respect for law enforcement and to be punctual. He taught kids who were members of the Safety Patrol Program that they were providing a service to the community and providing service to the community was important. All the kids knew and respected him and he always had time for them." The city's new police headquarters was named in Morken's honor in 2007.

Racism on the home front: A painstakingly documented overview of racism in the war industry on Puget Sound can be found in *Pacific Northwest Quarterly*, Fall 2007, Boeing Aircraft Company's Manpower Campaign during World War II, by Polly Reed Myers.

Other key reference works: *Washington, A Centennial History*, by Robert E. Ficken and Charles P. LeWarne (ISBN 0-295-96693-9); University of Washington Press, 1988. *The War Years, A Chronicle of Washington State in World War II*, by James R. Warren (ISBN 0-295-98076-1); University of Washington Press, 2000. A year-by-year overview of Home Front Washington.

Compelling interview: Charleen Burnette, public access manager and moderator for Bremerton Kitsap Access Television's "Around Kitsap" program, aired an interview with Lillian Walker and Linda Joyce on Aug. 29, 2008, as the Kitsap County YWCA celebrated its 60th anniversary. The videographer for BKAT was Michael R. Downum. **www.bkat.org**

Student project: Cecelia R. Walker, a student at Olympic College, interviewed Mrs. Walker in 2009 and wrote a warm profile for her class on "Women in American Culture." We thank her for sharing it.

BlackPast.org, a 3,000-page reference center on African American history; The web site director is Quintard Taylor, the Scott and Dorothy Bullitt Professor of American History at the University of Washington, Seattle. Link: **www.blackpast.org** **http://www.blackpast. org/?q=aaw/sinclair-park-kitsap-county-washington-1943-1948**

The Black Historical Society of Kitsap County:
http://www.kitsapblackhistory.org/

HistoryLink.org history of the Puget Sound Naval Shipyard:
http://www.historylink.org/index.cfm?DisplayPage=output.cfm&file_id=5579

Seattle Civil Rights & Labor History Project:
http://depts.washington.edu/civilr/

Seattle/King County NAACP:
http://jbible-naacp.blogspot.com/

A Washington State Bar Association article on a landmark
State Supreme Court case: Browning vs. Slenderella:
http://www.wsba.org/media/publications/barnews/
archives/2001/feb-01-segregation.htm

University of Washington Civil Rights and Labor History Project:
http://depts.washington.edu/civilr/mckinney.htm

DONORS

With gratitude to the following, whose generous gifts and assistance in fund-raising made possible the publication of this important book. Special thanks to the YWCA of Kitsap County, its Board and Executive Director, Linda K. Joyce, and to Judge J. Robin Hunt, who brought Mrs. Walker's inspirational life story to our attention. Many thanks to these contributors:

Carol Blakley

Natalie Bryson

Adele Ferguson Philipsen

Carolyn Hershberger

J. Robin Hunt

Ann Lovell

Katherine Smith

Marie Spearman

Marjorie Thorne

Gordon Walgren

Jan Williams

Sinclair Missionary Baptist Church

Ebenezer African Methodist Episcopal Church

Black Historical Society of Kitsap County

Washington State Heritage Center Trust

YWCA of Kitsap County

Q&A WITH LILLIAN WALKER

The happiest day of your life?

August 29, 1945, the day my son, James Titus Walker Jr., was born. I'd had problem pregnancies—lost three daughters—and he was a beautiful healthy, baby boy.

Your motto?

"The Golden Rule"—Luke 6:31: "Do unto others as you would have them do unto you." Practically every religion has some version of this. That's the way I work on anything I work on. If it's going to better you, it's going to better me.

Why are you always smiling?

Frowning and cursing won't make you any friends.

Favorite book?

The Bible. I keep it right by the bed. I like the Psalms.

The smartest thing you've ever done?

Marry James.

The dumbest?

Not follow my parents' teachings and going down the wrong path with the wrong people.

Favorite Movie?

"Gone with the Wind." Hattie McDaniel won an Oscar playing "Mammy." She was a black lady doing all the work and giving the best advice in that household.

Favorite recipe?

Chess Pie. It's the one I get the most compliments on. It's pretty much just butter, sugar, eggs and cream in a single crust. It's an old Southern tradition. I have a friend at church who always says, "Mrs. Walker when you feel up to it, I'm still waiting on my Chess Pie!" Here's the recipe: 2 cups sugar; 2 tablespoons flour; seven-eighths of a stick of butter; 3 eggs well beaten; 1 cup evaporated milk; 1 teaspoon lemon extract. In a mixing bowl beat the eggs; add the other ingredients; pour into unbaked pie shell then sprinkle with a little corn meal; bake in a 400-degree oven for 40 minutes; reduce heat to 300 degrees and continue baking 15 or 20 minutes or until knife inserted in center of pie comes out clean.

What's your idea of an ideal day?

To wake up and thank the Lord that He's brought me through the night again and just to have friends call and just be glad you're alive.

INDEX